C000185934

Hg2|Johannesburg

Forum Homini

# Hg2|Johannesburg

# How to…

*A Hedonist's guide to Johannesburg* is broken down into easy to use sections: Sleep, Eat, Drink, Snack, Party, Culture, Shop, Play and Info. In each section you'll find detailed reviews and photographs. At the front of the book is an introduction to Johannesburg and an overview map, followed by introductions to the main areas and more detailed maps. On each of these maps the places we have featured are laid out by section, highlighted on the map with a symbol and a number. To find out about a particular place simply turn to the relevant section, where all entries are listed alphabetically. Alternatively, browse through a specific section (e.g. Eat) until you find a restaurant you like the look of. Surrounding your choice will be a coloured box – each colour refers to a particular area of the Johannesburg. Simply turn to the relevant map to find the location.

# Book your hotel on Hg2.com

We believe that the key to a great Johannesburg break is choosing the right hotel. Our unique site now enables you to browse through our selection of hotels, using the interactive maps to give you a good feel for the area as well as the nearby restaurants, bars, sights, etc., before you book. Hg2 has formed partnerships with the hotels featured in our guide to bring them to readers at the lowest possible price. Our site now incorporates special offers from selected hotels, as well information on new openings.

# The concept

*A Hedonist's guide to Johannesburg* is designed to appeal to quirky, urbane and the incredibly stylish traveller. The kind of person interested in viewing the city from a different angle – someone who feels the need to explore, shop and play away from the crowds of tourists and become part of one of the city's many scenes. We give you an insider's knowledge of Johannesburg; Andrew wants to make you feel like an in-the-know local, and take you to the hottest places in town (both above and under ground) to rub shoulders with the scenesters and glitterati alike.

Work so often rules our life, and weekends away are few and far between; when we do manage to break away we want to have as much fun and to relax as much as possible with the minimum amount of stress. This guide is all about maximizing time. The photographs of every place we feature help you to make a quick choice and fit in with your own style.

A Hedonist's guide to…

# Johannesburg

Written by
Andrew Ludwig

A Hedonist's Guide to Johannesburg

Written by
Andrew Ludwig

Additional Research and Writing by
Kiki Spiers and Shan Pascall

Photographed by
Andrew Ludwig and Graham Springer

Edited by
Nick Clarke, Tremayne Carew Pole, Eleanor Aldridge

Managing director – Tremayne Carew Pole
Design – Nick Randall
Maps – Amber Sheers & Nick Randall
Repro – Advantage Digital Print
Printer – Leo Paper
Publisher – Filmer Ltd

Email – info@hg2.com
Website – www.hg2.com

Published in the United Kingdom in June 2010 by
Filmer Ltd
17 Shawfield Street
London SW3 4BA

ISBN – 978-1-905428-48-9

Unlike many other nameless guidebooks we pride ourselves on our independence and our integrity. We eat in all the restaurants, drink in all the bars, and go wild in the nightclubs – all totally incognito. We charge no one for the privilege of appearing in the guide, and every place is reviewed and included at our discretion.

Cities are best enjoyed by soaking up the atmosphere: wander the streets, partake in some retail therapy, re-energize yourself with a massage and then get ready to revel in Johannesburg's nightlife until dawn.

# Hg2 Johannesburg author

### Andrew Ludwig

Andrew is a native Jozi, although like many South Africans of his generation he has travelled extensively around the world. As a part time journalist and entrepreneur he understands businesses from both sides, providing excellent objectivity. His businesses are travel orientated with his most enjoyable one being a fly-fishing enterprise taking small groups of dedicated fishermen around the world. Although he spends less time than he would like at home returning to Jo'burg and re-exploring the city's nefarious delights and happening on exciting new places.

# ■ Johannesburg

Jo'burg – more commonly referred to as 'Jozi' – is finally shedding its fierce reputation as a notorious no-go area and attracting a new breed of adventurous visitors by the planeload. Nowadays visitors aren't just using the city as a transfer point to other parts of South Africa, but are actually leaving the confines of the airport, checking into hotels and experiencing Jo'burg as a destination in itself. As they should, since Jo'burg – the largest city in South Africa and the provincial capital of Gauteng, South Africa's richest province– is truly worthy some exploration.

Having long played a beauty and the beast-type role in the worldwide media – sadly known more for its crime rate than its cityscape – Jo'burg is, in fact, a city you should see before you die rather than a city you go to die in. Crime is indeed high here – we're not going to beat around the African bush – but armed with knowledge and common sense (as opposed to AK-47s), visitors should feel as safe here as they do in any other major city. It's simple; don't carry valuables around with you; don't walk about alone or at night, particularly in the CBD; and don't leave car doors unlocked, especially at traffic lights. You can't plan everything, of course, but by sticking to a few simple rules you can minimise the risk to yourself and get the very best out of Jo'burg. Experiencing the beauty rather than the beast, as it were.

Statistically, Jo'burg is home to around four million inhabitants and boasts one of the mildest climates in the world. Never too hot or humid, summer days are usually warm and wind-free while winter days are crisp and clear – perfect for those pounding the pavements in search of all that the city has to offer. Founded after the discovery of ore in the region, the city is built on mining. Commerce eventually arrived in the CBD, but this soon dissolved after crime consumed the district and businesses decided to move to other suburbs. Competition among illegal immigrants is fierce, and is forcing many to turn to a life of crime for survival. That said, as with most of Jo'burg, efforts are being made to regenerate the area – both architecturally and economically – to coincide with the FIFA 2010 World Cup.

Despite being large and sprawling, Jo'burg's makeup isn't that hard to work out. Old gold and diamond mines make up the outskirts, while the inner-city area of the

CBD is characterised by buildings that punctuate the sky like daggers; its many-faceted suburbs, from Sandton to Fourways, make up the rest of this beating, buzzing metropolis. Many of Jo'burg's more affluent residents live in Sandton, with the city's population a melting pot of cultures this makes for a cosmopolitan, diverse environment. The majority of the city's four- and five-star hotels are located in Sandton, which is where most people stay when in town; visitors are unlikely to travel far through unchartered, seemingly hostile territory, and for this reason many of the recommendations in this guide are based in and around this busy area. Here, Jo'burg's elite lives behind in gated communities behind high walls, while the majority live in less salubrious settlements dotted around the city. Luxury cars jostle against bangers on the streets, while designer shops and trendy restaurants jar against stalls and street vendors.

Sights, too, can be found in the area, with Jo'burg's colourful history traced through its landscape and cultural offerings. Highly recommended is a tour of Jo'burg's various townships and museums, ensuring that culture vultures are kept safe while soaking it all up.

Sport is big business here, too, with cricket and golf something of national treasures. Football and rugby are also enjoyed, while horse racing is beloved among those who can afford to hedge their bets. For the more extreme, the city also offers adrenaline-pumping sports such as bungee jumping and 'kloofing' – making your way down a waterway without a boat. As active or as laid-back as you are, Jo'burg has things to do for all types of travellers.

Formerly a city that only received press when something bad was going on, it's comforting to know that good things occur in Jo'burg, too. Regeneration is sweeping away urban decay suburb by suburb, while Jo'burg's many scars – physical, social and economic – are healing. Slowly, perhaps, but surely.

# Johannesburg Overview

## Sleep

1. 10 2nd Avenue
2. Fairlawns
3. Forum Homini
4. InterContinental – Airport
5. The Orient

## Eat

6. Angie's
7. Casalinga
8. Mosaic
9. Roots

## Drink

10. Radium Beerhall
11. Troyeville Hotel

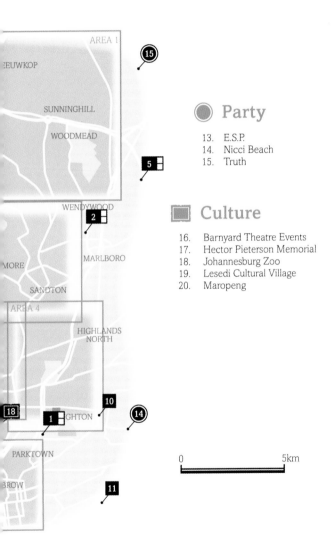

## Party

13. E.S.P.
14. Nicci Beach
15. Truth

## Culture

16. Barnyard Theatre Events
17. Hector Pieterson Memorial
18. Johannesburg Zoo
19. Lesedi Cultural Village
20. Maropeng

0　　　　　　　　　5km

# Central Business District,
*Newtown, Braamfontein, Hillbrow & Yeoville*

The Central Business District – more commonly called Johannesburg CBD – is the main business district of the city, and houses the densest population of gleaming skyscrapers in Africa. The Carlton Centre Office Tower is the tallest building on the continent, in fact, and rises 730-foot into the skyline. With its reputation often preceding it, the CBD has been notorious for violence and urban decay; many white South Africans have left the area for safer neighbourhoods in the northern suburbs, leaving buildings empty and open to vandalism and squatting. A collision of the first and third worlds, the streets of the CBD are now lined with traders flogging their wares – from brightly-coloured fruit to even more brightly-coloured clothes. Office workers toting Starbucks cups have since moved on.

That said, the CBD has seen something of a revival in recent years and is home to number of noteworthy sites should you pay a visit; highlights include the Johannesburg Art Gallery and the SAB World of Beer. The Standard Bank Collection of African Art is also worth checking out for aesthetes. As with any downtown neighbourhood in any city, be wary of your personal belongings – daylight muggings aren't uncommon, and visitors should be particularly careful when withdrawing money from cash points or snapping photos with flashy cameras. And don't even think about heading into the CBD by night without taxi transportation there and back. Pound the pavements in groups and steer clear of quiet areas; if travelling by rented car, ensure you keep your doors locked at all times – especially when stopping at traffic lights.

Surrounding areas include Newton, Braamfontein, Hillbrow and Yeoville. Newton is to the west of the CBD, and is marked by the hustle and bustle of the Market Theatre Precinct with an assorted mix of shops, bars and galleries. Braamfontein straddles Jan Smuts Avenue and Empire Road and is connected to the city by Nelson Mandela Bridge; as a hub of arts and entertainment, theatregoers should check out The Johannesburg Civic Centre. Hillbrow is a residential neighbourhood known for its unemployment, poverty and crime; poor infrastructure and lack of investment have left a chaotic slum of street markets and ramshackle houses in its path. Urban regeneration is underway, however. Yeoville, meanwhile, was originally marketed as a 'sanitarium for the rich' but has attracted a mix of classes instead. Located on a ridge overlooking the city – for cleaner air, apparently – Yeoville is another area to undergo regeneration.

# Central Business District,
## Newtown, Braamfontein, Hillbrow & Yeoville

**Sleep**

1.   The Westcliff Hotel

**Eat**

2.   Gramadoelas
3.   La Belle Terrase

**Drink**

4.   Polo Lounge
at the Westcliff

**Snack**

5.   The Conservatory

**Party**

6.   Bassline

**Culture**

7.   Constitution Hill
8.   Johannesburg
Civic Theatre
9.   Market Theatre

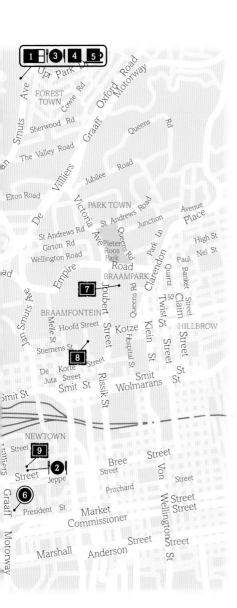

0             1km

# ■ Sandton

As the 90210 of Johannesburg, so to speak, Sandton takes its name from the two separate suburbs of Sandown and Bryanston (although Bryanston has now been merged with Johannesburg to become part of the City of Johannesburg Metropolitan Municipality rather than a suburb of Sandton). While it can no longer claim to be an independent town as it could during Apartheid, Sandton is still the most pleasant area to live and work in Johannesburg. In fact, Sandton is the city's premier business district since office workers fled the CBD in favour of a more secure suburb – and quite rightly so! Indeed, violence is kept to a minimum here and business can generally be conducted without fear or looking over sharp-suited shoulders; this is, in large part, thanks to the high number of CCTV cameras dotted about its streets.

So successful has this area been in fostering business, that Sandton is undergoing a multi-billion rand upgrade that includes an 80-storey officer tower – built to replace the largely abandoned and iconic Carlton Centre in the CBD. No doubt the many banks and financial consultants based close by will once again start to feel at home here staring down at the city beneath them and providing the area with a visual focal point.

Residents, too, are drawn to Sandton for the higher quality of life than in Johannesburg's poorer suburbs; dubbed 'Africa's richest square mile', this prestigious piece of land is so popular that there's not much space left to build. As a result, recent development has reached for the skies with buildings such as Michelangelo

Towers offering would-be residents luxurious living space above-sea-level. The only way is up, apparently, and locals are going willingly.

Other than office and residential space, Sandton is made up of retail outlets – and plenty of them. One of Sandton's main attractions is Sandton City; as one of the largest shopping centres in South Africa, together with Nelson Mandela Square, it's where cards are maxed out and style snapped up. Visitors can shop 'til they drop here, with over 300 shops to splurge in from Armani through to Cartier. Naturally, a collection of suitably stylish restaurants and cafés cater to shoppers looking to refuel after a strenuous day pounding the pavement.

Another of the area's draws is the Sandton Convention Centre; as the largest on the continent, it's little wonder its hosted events such as the World Summit on Sustainable Development and the African National Congress's victory celebrations. And as you'd expect for such a hive of activity, Sandton is home to a string of fabulous five-star hotels in which weary travellers can rest their bodies between fine thread-count sheets.

# Sandton

## Sleep

1. AtholPlace
2. Balalaika
3. The Falstaff
4. The Michelangelo
5. The Quatermain
6. The Saxon

## Eat

7. The Baron Sandown
8. Beirut
9. Ghazal
10. The Saxon
11. Thomas Maxwell
12. Wang Thai

## Drink

13. Baron Sandown

## Snack

14. Andicco 24
15. Annica's Deli
16. Bella
17. Life
18. The Saxon
19. Tasha's Cafe - Atholl
20. Tasha's Cafe - Morning Side
21. Vida E

## Party

22. The Blues Room
23. Fashion TV Cafe
24. Taboo

## Shop

27. Morningside Shopping Centre
28. Sandton City
29. Sandton Square

## Culture

25. Old Mutual Theatre
26. Ster Kinekor

# Bryanston, Rivonia & Fourways

A suburb of the upper-classes, Bryanston takes its name from a village in Dorset and is a largely residential area. Split into two parts by Bryanston Drive, which runs from the edge of Randburg to Morningside, it is home to an array of fabulous houses as well as number of stylish shopping and dining options.

The Bryanston Shopping Centre caters to the area's affluent residents with 55 stores offering designers goods galore; coffee shops and restaurants add to its appeal on the corner of William Nicol Drive and Ballyclare Avenue.

And if this stylish mall caters to Bryanston's ladies-that-lunch, then nearby Bryanston Country Club targets Bryanston's hedonistic husbands; founded back in 1948, the country club has been a centre of sport and social events since its inception and has more than 2,000 well-heeled members in its exclusive database. Complete with gorgeous greens for serious golfers, only the cream of the city-based crop congregates here.

Yet another of Jo'burg's affluent Suburbs is Rivonia. Straddling Braamfontein Spruit and Sandspruit, Rivonia is historically known as the location of Liliesleaf Farm – where many of those involved in the Rivonia Treason Trial were arrested

(when 19 senior ANC leaders were charged with treason as a mechanism to break up and silence the organisation). Nowadays its best known as the home of both business and pleasure. Rivonia Boulevard is where locals come to shop – either at Rivonia Square or the Rivonia Village shopping malls – while other areas give way to massive mansions and oversized offices.

As one of Jo'burg's fastest-growing areas, Fourways is a suburb to watch; located to the north of Sandton, it was named after its convenient position on four major crossroads. Indeed, as the name suggests, it's easy to reach from whichever side of the city you're coming from.

Fourways Mall and the factory outlet-style Fourways Crossing act as the commercial hub of the suburb, while a number of hip and happening restaurants, bars and clubs attract the young and trendy. The MonteCasino also draws big spenders; decked out in a faux-Tuscan style, it's gimmicks and gambling at its most fun.

# Bryanston, Rivonia & Fourways

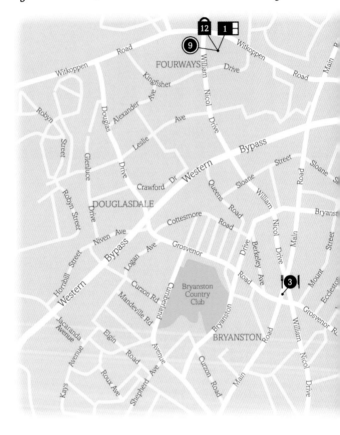

| | Sleep | | | Eat | | | Snac |
|---|---|---|---|---|---|---|---|
| 1. | Palazzo Montecasino | | 3. | Col'Cacchio | | 5. | Contessa |
| 2. | Tintswalo at Waterfall | | 4. | Rocket | | | |

0           1km

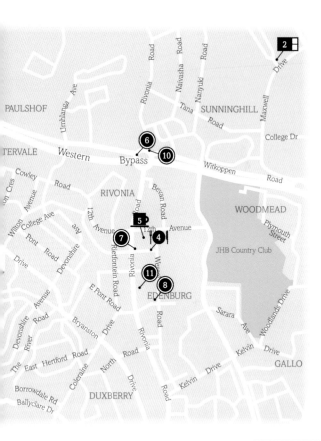

## ● Party

6. Fashion TV Cafe
7. The Grand
8. The Manhattan Club
9. Montecasino
10. Movida
11. Teazers Rivonia

## ▮ Shop

12. Montecasino

# Parkhurst & Saxonwold

Small but densely populated, the suburb of Parkhurst is located to the north of Jo'burg and is predominantly residential. 4th Avenue is the main commercial area, and is lined with more than enough restaurants, cafés and shops to keep visitors spending their hard-earned Rand; 6th Street, meanwhile, is fast becoming a major design district, with a number of art galleries and concept design stores seemingly opening their doors by the day.

Street culture is big in Parkhurst, as you can imagine, and al fresco fun is definitely the way forward; with so many sidewalk cafes, bars and restaurants offering outside space to their customers, it's an extremely social suburb indeed with an open, friendly atmosphere as unacquainted Jozis catch up on city gossip. With a village-like ambience upheld by the local resident's association, it's nice to see such a quaint, friendly neighbourhood in such a vast, sprawling city.

Saxonworld, meanwhile, is made up of Parkview, Westcliff and Houghton, and is one of the most picturesque areas of the city – as well as being one of the oldest. Broad, tree-lined streets wind their way through lush greenery, while sedate neighbourhoods abound. A key attraction in this area is Johannesburg Zoo – a 45-hectare park in the heart of Parktown – while the shopping centres of Rosebank and Hyde Park are close by. Once again, Saxonworld fosters a social pavement culture, with lunches being enjoyed outside its cafes and al fresco liquid sustenance outside its bars. With a heady nightlife to boot, revellers need no encouragement to fall out of its clubs and onto its pavements after booze-fuelled evenings out on the tiles.

# Parkhurst and Saxonwold

## Sleep

1. The Grace
2. Monarch Hotel
3. The Rosebank
4. Ten Bompas Road
5. Southern Sun Hyde Park

## Eat

6. The Attic
7. Espresso Caffe
8. Fino
9. The Grillhouse
10. Louis XVI
11. Turn 'n Tender
12. Wombles

## Drink

13. The Attic
14. The Circle Bar
15. Espresso Caffe
16. Fino
17. Giles
18. Hyde Park Hotel Bar
19. Jolly Cool
20. The Jolly Rodger
21. Katzy's

## Snack

22. Andiccio 24
23. Chocodore
24. I Love Cup Cakes
25. Moemas Pastma
26. Stephanie's
27. Vida E - Greenside
28. Vida E - Parktown
29. Wild Olive

0           1km

HYDE PARK

William Nicol Drive

Waterfall Ave

Smuts

2nd Rd

Rosebank Road

Morsim

1st Road

Norfolk

Northumberland Ave

Smuts Avenue

North Rd

Bompas Road

Kent Road

Hume Road

Smits Road

Eastwood Road

Christopherson Road

Cradock Ave

Jellicoe Avenue

Oxford Road

ROSEBANK

7th Ave

Bolton Road

## ◉ Party

30.   Gin
31.   Latinova
32.   Moloko
33.   Tokyo Star

## ▦ Culture

34.   Cinema Nouveau
35.   Everard Read Gallery
36.   Goodman Gallery
37.   Nu Metro Cinema

## ▤ Shop

38.   Hyde Park
      Shopping Centre
39.   Mall of Rosebank
40.   4th Avenue

# Illovo & Melrose

Bordering Hyde Park, Sandhurst and Craighall Park, Illovo is one of Jo'burg's most prestigious suburbs. And thanks to the famous Wanderers Stadium, which can found here, one of the most talked-about, too. Home to Jo'burg's resident cricket team, the Highveld Strikers, the stadium is dubbed 'The Bullring' thanks to its circular design and can accommodate up to 34,000 cheering fans. And next to this is the equally famous Wanderers Golf Course, comprising 18 holes and lush, undulating greens. Indeed, sport is one of Illovo's defining features.

But it's not all about a game only the former members of the British empire understands and golf, Illovo is also locally known as the place to come for hip restaurants, bars and shops. With many of its venue placing an emphasis on design, it truly caters to its well-heeled residents and trendy visitors.

The nearby suburb of Melrose is distinctly upmarket, too, with an ever-expanding commercial sector and plenty of gorgeous hotels to house its visitors in. The area is now characterised by Melrose Arch, a contemporary leisure/business complex built to mimic the architecture of a European street. It is also home to Melrose Arch Hotel, one of Jo'burg's flashiest new design hotels.

# Ilovo and Melrose

## ▮▮ Sleep

1. Melrose Arch Hotel
2. The Peech

## |●| Eat

3. Assaggi
4. Faff
5. Fishmonger
6. Mezepoli
7. Moyo
8. Plaka

## ▮ Drink

9. Pool & Library Bar
   - Melrose Arch Hotel

## Snack

10. Red Mango
11. Tashas

## Party

12. Rose Boys

## Shop

13. Birdhaven
14. Blu Bird Shopping Centre
15. Central Avenue
16. Melrose Arch

# sleep…

Over the past decade Jo'burg has benefited from South Africa's growth as a global player in the tourism industry and as a much sought after business destination. South Africa, and more specifically Jo'burgs popularity has been largely reinforced by the numerous sporting events and conferences that have taken place in the country and in anticipation of the FIFA 2010 World Cup. The preparation for major events has ensured that the country's infrastructure has been both elevated and revolutionised. Noticeable improvements to the transport system, airports and the service and hospitality sector make for a seemingly hassle free trip into the 'dark' continent. The top hotel chains have all established a presence, while many stylish boutique hotels have popped up around the city providing visitors with charming, small alternatives often imbued with a uniquely African touch.

South Africa's new found dynamism has realised a diverse selection of hotels in the 'rainbow nation'. Most are established within close proximity to the shopping centres abundant in Jo'burg,  which accommodate not only shops but restaurants and bars giving sometimes slightly nervous visitors the ideal safe and secure hospitality experience.

We have elected to focus on hotels in the Sandton area of Jo'burg. Primarily, this is largely because the majority are concentrated here, but also because the diversity will appeal to business and leisure traveller alike. The principal suburbs include Rosebank, Melrose, Hyde Park, Fourways and the Sandton Central node. All these suburbs are simply linked to shopping centres and their attendant restaurants and bars are a short drive or walk away.

If you are a little worried about the security situation then chauffer services and taxis are available from all hotels upon request and will ensurea seemless transfer to the restaurant or bar of your choice.

All recommendations make provision for the business traveller, offering conference facilities, meeting rooms as well as business centres for those of you travelling sans hardware. All hotels have internet access, most of which is Wi-Fi, although you will sadly notice Southern African connectivity is not quite of the same speed experienced in the rest of the world.

The rates given range from the price of a double room in low season to the price of a suite in high season. High season runs from November through to March.

Ten Bompas

sleep...

Athol Place

# the best hotels

Top ten:
1. The Saxon
2. The Peech
3. The Michelangelo
4. The Westcliff
5. Fairlawns
6. The Monarch
7. The Orient
8. AtholPlace
9. The Grace
10. Palazzo Montecasino

Style:
1. The Saxon
2. The Westcliff
3. The Peech
4. The Orient
5. The Michelangelo

Atmosphere:
1. The Saxon
2. The Michelangelo
3. Melrose Arch
4. The Grace
5. The Orient

Location:
1. The Michelangelo
2. The Saxon
3. The Grace
4. The Melrose Arch
5. Southern Sun Hyde Park

### 2nd Avenue Houghton Estate
*(top-left)*

10 2nd Avenue,
Houghton Estate, Houghton
Tel: 011 853 2400
www.houghtonestate.com
Rates: R1,345–4,100

With just 14 rooms the affordably grand Houghton Estate, reminiscent of an English country house, is a true boutique hotel. Beloved of international luminaries ranging from Sir Richard Branson to Kofi Annan the hotel is found in the wealthy suburb of Houghton, home to Nelson Mandela and many of Jo'burg's movers and shakers. The classic interior décor is suitably refined, with comfortable bedrooms, intimate public spaces and a wide veranda opening up onto the verdant gardens. A small kitchen caters to guests providing breakfast, dinner and light lunches on request; while those in need of a drink, if the free soft drink mini bar won't suffice, can retire to the cocktail bar or explore the well-stocked wine cellar. The discreet conference facilities make Houghton Estate the perfect place for high level meetings and corporate events.

**Style 8, Atmosphere 7, Location 7**

### AtholPlace
*(right)*

90 Pretoria Avenue
(off Katherine Street) Atholl
Tel: 011 783 3410
www.atholplace.co.za
Rates: R2,500–3,500

Situated only 30 minutes from OR Tambo International Airport and within close proximity of Sandton Central, guests have access to some of the city's finest shopping and an abundance of restaurants and bars to keep hedonists going all night. With only ten suites AtholPlace is definitely boutique in feel – each of the rooms is uniquely decorated, although they all contain the same menu of luxe trappings (Frette linen, deep duck-down duvets, 42-inch flatscreens) and there is a meticulous attention to detail throughout. The overall feel is difficult to describe landing somewhere between neo-colonial and rustic chic. Outside the Afrikaans origins are apparent and a beautiful garden surrounds the hotel and the large swimming pool, where guests unwind. A small in-house kitch-

en caters solely to the guests and free pre-prandial drinks are served in the evening – it almost feels like a rather smart house party, but don't worry you can be as anti-social as you like.

**Style 8, Atmosphere 7, Location 9**

**The Balalaika** *(bottom-left)*
Maude Street, Sandton,
Village Walk, Gauteng,
Tel: 011 322 5000
www.balalaika.co.za
Rates: R1,200–1,530

Neither the most opulent nor the most expensive hotel in Sandton, the four-star Balalaika is included because it is affordable and good value for money, especially for the hedonist who wants to live like a rock star, but may not exactly have the pay packet. Centrally located, next to the Village Walk shopping centre and opposite the Johannesburg Securities Exchange, there are a few shops, cinemas and restaurants nearby or it's just a short walk to Sandton City. The 330 rooms (yes, it's pretty damn big) range from comfortably basic to, well, comfortably basic. There is a garden, swimming pool and gym to unwind in or for those who enjoy a drink the Lord's Bar is English pub-like (well, sort of) – but it does get busy (and buzzy) in the evenings – a coffee shop and a pool bar for long soaking-up-the-rays lunches.

**Style 7, Atmosphere 7, Location 8**

---

### The Fairlawns *(left)*
### Boutique Hotel & Spa

1 Alma Rd off Bowling Ave, Morningside
Tel: 082 602 6112 www.fairlawns.co.za
Rates: R2,920–21,780

Once the property of the Oppenheimer Family, the impressive Fairlawns Boutique Hotel & Spa has been lovingly and lavishly refurbished. More of a country house hotel than an urban retreat, there are 12 courtyard suites, all individually decorated and monikered The Bismark or The English Manor, with the Honeymoon Suite having a reproduction four poster from Versailles. The six beautifully designed premier suites fuse styles from around the world, twisting them with a modern touch. Surrounding the rooms are sprawling lawns, perfectly manicured gardens and a swimming pool. Breakfast, lunch and dinner can be taken on the Italian influenced terrace during the summer and to counteract those surprisingly chilly winter nights a roaring fire in the bar keeps drinkers warm. A Balinese-style spa re-energises and relaxes before venturing out into the hustle and bustle of the city. Conveniently situated in the Sandton suburb of Morningside Manor the major business hubs and shopping centers are just a short taxi ride away.

**Style 9, Atmosphere 8, Location 8**

### The Falstaff *(middle)*
223 Rivonia Road,
Morningside, Sandton
Tel: 011 784 8580   www.falstaff.co.za
Rates: R1,087–1,498

Harking back to a bygone era the Falstaff embraces a warming English nostalgia. The interior design appears to have been lifted from a 1950's country house hotel, complete with the floral furniture covers The 41 rooms are comfortable but intrinsically unexciting, they might be a little too corporate for some; however, they are affordable and definitely good value for money. A sun trap courtyard swimming pool is the perfect place to grab a coffee and a few rays. The in-house Italian restaurant is unremarkable but they do serve a good full English breakfast. Right in centre of Sandton the hotel is perfect for business travellers and shopaholics alike (well, Village Walk, Nelson Mandela Square and Sandton City – see Shop – are all within five minutes.

**Style 7, Atmosphere 7, Location 9**

### Forum Homini *(right)*
Letamo Game Estate, Barlet
Road, (off Ventersdorp Road/N14),
Krugersdorp
Tel: 011 668 7000
www.forumhomini.co.za
Rates: R3,500

Set within a private game estate in one of the world's natural heritage sites – just 40 minutes from Jo'burg and Pretoria – Forum Homini offers an interesting take on the traditional game farm. The essence is based on the evolution of nature and its entrance incorporates a giant sculpture depicting the transformation of the human skull, a reference to the area's moniker as 'The Cradle of Mankind', after the discovery of very early civilization nearby. The 12 luxury suites, honeymoon and presidential suites sit in the protective arm of a shallow basin, blending into the environment with their stone walls, grass roofs overlooking a natural watering hole. The suites are built for romance with roaring fires, canopied beds and double baths overlooking the

veld. Stalactite lights rise from the floor and outdoor showers complete the return to nature. The area itself offers a myriad of attractions such as the Maropeng, Sterkfontein Caves, the Lion and Rhino Nature Reserve, Wonder Caves Observatory, to name but a few.

**Style 8, Atmosphere 8, Location 6**

...................................................

**The Grace** *(top)*
54 Bath Avenue, Rosebank
Tel: 011 280 7200 www.thegrace.co.za
Rates: R2,375–2,909

The Grace is one of those hotels in Jo'burg that's revered by locals and visitors alike. Just missing out on the boutique tag, the 73 rooms are a little north of that, the hotel neatly transects the business/leisure divide. Although the presence of trouser presses in the rooms hints at the former and a throw back to a past decade, while the décor seems to appeal more to a slightly gentrified, shuffleboard crowd. The Dining Room, under the watchful gaze of Chef Doctor Hlongwane, has, in previous days, been voted one of South Africa's top ten restaurants. A fourth floor roof terrace overlooks the leafy, mature garden, mamba-green lawn, jacaranda trees and swimming pool – sipping strawberry daiquiris up here is the perfect end to a busy day. For those who need to break out a sky walk connects the hotel to the Rosebank Mall and a whole host of retail therapy.

**Style 8, Atmosphere 8, Location 7**

...................................................

**InterContinental** *(middle)*
O R Tambo International
Airport, Jo'burg
Tel: 011 961 5400
www.southernsun.com
Rates: R3,250–15,000

South Africa's first and only luxury airport hotel, the InterContinental Jo'burg O.R. Tambo Airport is conveniently located within walking distance from the terminals. More of a transit hotel the InterCon is never going to set the world on fire, but it will cater to your needs for a few passing hours. There is a 24 hour gym with all the toys, an indoor heated pool, and a Camelot spa. The rooms are typical of the group: comfortable, reasonably spacious but just lacking in charm. They are quiet and completely soundproofed with double glazed windows. The Quills restaurant is well regarded for producing a modern take on international cooking and has an outdoor terrace for those warm summer evenings. The InterCon is a choice for convenience to the airport and not a place to choose to be in the hub of city life.

**Style 7, Atmosphere 6, Location 6**

...................................................

**The Melrose** *(bottom)*
**Arch Hotel**
1 Melrose Square,
Melrose Arch
Tel: 011 214 6666
www.africanpridehotels.com
Rates: from R2,055

The Melrose Arch Hotel is found in the burgeoning Melrose Arch lifestyle development. A city within a city

designed to give security to Johannesburg's growing middle and upper classes; the entire precinct is patrolled by 24 hour security and surveillance. This is the new South Africa. However, politics aside, this five-star hotel is a temple to 21st Century urban design padded out with creature comforts and little added luxuries. The in-house March restaurant (See Eat) follows the Jo'burg trend of pandering to their international guests and producing good eclectic cooking. Alongside this is a 'deluxe' Library bar (see Drink) complete with billiard (well pool, really) table and an outdoor pool bar for lazy summer afternoon cocktails. Laid back for a business hotel and grown up for a leisure hotel the Melrose Arch is part of a new breed of sophisticated Jo'burg properties.

**Style 9, Atmosphere 8, Location 8**

**The Michelangelo Hotel** *(top)*
135 West Street,
Nelson Mandela Square, Sandton
Tel: 011 282 7000
www.michelangelo.co.za
Rates: R2,550–2,990

One of the more impressive and elegant hotels in the city, The Michelangelo, a member of 'Leading Hotels of the World', is often seen as one of Jo'burg's grande dames. The impressive double height lobby wows new visitors on arrival and sets the tone of things to come. The charming Il Ritrovo lounge offers tapas-style dining around a focal grand piano, while the Piccolo Mondo is chef Andrew Atkinson's pride and joy. The rooms, although comfortable and kitted out with all the toys, are slightly bland and just a little too mid-range corporate in design. The location is one of Michelangelo's key selling points, right in the heart of one of Africa's most exclusive shopping centres, Nelson Mandela Square, there's a good choice of restaurants, bars, shops, as well as cinemas and theatres on its doorstep.

**Style 8, Atmosphere 8, Location 9**

**The Monarch** *(bottom)*
167 Oxford Road,
Rosebank, Sandton
Tel: 011 341 2000
www.monarchhotels.co.za
Rates: R4,000–23,000

The Monarch is housed within a beautiful listed building – well the old Post Office actually – the interior of which was lovingly transformed in 2006. The decor fuses contemporary touches (Frette linens and WiFi) with period elegance (free standing baths and vintage furniture) and is nostalgically reminiscent of a bygone era. The Monarch prides itself on its gastronomic and artistic flair. The restaurant, under the watchful eye of Chef Keith Frisely, is well-known for its tasting menus and modern take on South African cuisine. While on the artistic side the hotel is home to an extensive collection of contemporary and classic South African art. The unheralded Oxford Street location, slap bang in the middle of the bustling suburb of Rosebank is within easy reach of some of Jo'burg's best shopping and dining.

**Style 9, Atmosphere 7, Location 8**

### The Orient  *(middle)*

Francolin Conservancy,
Elandsfontein, Crocodile River Valley
Tel: 012 371 2902
www.the-orient.net
Rates: R2,800–4,000

Building on the success of its restaurant, Mosaic (see Eat) – recently awarded the title of South Africa's best restaurant, The Orient's reputation is growing in stature. Situated in the *veld,* just 40 minutes from Sandton, it is a homage to the Middle East and might be more at home in an exclusive suburb of Marrakech or Damascus than Johannesburg. Set amid paved terraces and palm trees, the Moorish style incorporates castellated walls and towers, replete with beautifully intricate woodwork and balconies. Inside, there are twelve suites taking their name from sub-continent, North African and Silk Route trading posts, each are furnished individually, with the antiques and hand-crafted furniture bearing a loose connection to their eponymous locations. A swimming pool, private cinema, croquet lawn and private balconies complete the swanky boutique feel. But, as we mentioned at the outset, the real attraction is the Mosaic restaurant, done up like a North African kasbah, where supreme international cooking is complimented by a 15,000 bottle wine cellar.

**Style 9, Atmosphere 8, Location 7**

### Palazzo Montecasino  *(left)*

Montecasino Boulevard,
Fourways, Sandton
Tel: 011 510 3000
www.palazzo-montecasino.com
Rates: R2,500

The Palazzo Montecasino is part of the Montecasino entertainment centre, incorporating a casino, aviary, cinemas, shops, theatres, restaurants and bars. The whole shebang has been built in a Tuscan style (the Gauteng lot really do love their themes), however, the Mon-

tecasino manages to carry it off without appearing overly kitsch. The 246 rooms are simple, elegant and stylish, kitted out with all the toys international travellers have come to expect. The Medeo restaurant is, unsurprisingly, Tuscan and uses herbs taken from their own garden. While the hotel is connected to the 'entertainment for the masses' complex the Palazzo retains a tranquil air, largely brought about by the stunning gardens complete with a vast ornamental koi pond and swimming pool from which to escape the heat of the sun. Despite its imposing and rather sophisticated grandeur the mood is relaxed and seems a world away from the centre of town.

**Style 7, Atmosphere 7, Location 8**

**The Peech** *(right)*
61 North Street, Melrose, Sandton
Tel: 011 537 979 www.thepeech.co.za
Rates: R1,750–2,050

Described as 'contemporary, edgy and Afro-centric' by Condé Nast Traveller and nominated as South Africa's leading boutique hotel for the last two consecutive years. The Peech provides hip, eco-sensitive, urbane travellers with an ideal hangout. Located in Jo'burg's upmarket suburb of Melrose, the hotel's sixteen bedrooms, spread around the garden, contrast modern design with traditional African wall hangings and animal skins. A bistro, manned by chef Greg Jardim, produces delicious local fare, with the herbs coming direct from the hotel's own small organic kitchen garden. The sustainable focus of the hotel is very *du jour*, water is recycled and solar power provides the heating for the water, and if that wasn't enough R5 from every guest night is donated to a local children's charity. A swimming pool provides a focus for guests to unwind and free WiFi means even the suits can chill in the sun.

**Style 9, Atmosphere 8, Location 8**

■ **The Quatermain**   *(top-left)*
60 West Road South,
Morningside, Sandton
Tel: 011 290 0900
www.quatermain.co.za
Rates: R1,287–3,432

Slap bang in the middle of Sandton the Quartermain is a more charming version of it's sibling property, The Falstaff. The grandiose building is inspired by the British architect Sir Edwin Lutyens, and takes his attachment to the country house and updates and transforms it to a contemporary South African style. The 102 rooms and two suites are warm and genteel in character, further expanding the country house theme. Stuffed to the gunnels with modcons, the rooms are perfect for the upscale business traveller.

Charming gardens surround the swimming pool and a shaded courtyard provides respite from the heat of the African sun. There is a restaurant on the premisis but to be frank it would be better to explore a little further afield, after all the hotel is not far from the central hub of Sandton and all the attendant bars and restaurants.

**Style 7, Atmosphere 7, Location 9**

........................................................

■ **The Rosebank**   *(bottom-left)*
CNR Tyrwhitt
& Sturdee Avenues, Rosebank
Tel: 011 448 3600
www.therosebank.co.za
Rates: R1,450–6,140

Part of the Crowne Plaza hotel chain

(but don't get put off by this, they have made leaps and bounds in recent years), The Rosebank is a modern and stylish addition for the modern, sophisticated corporate traveller (also perfect if you're a sportsfan – Ellis Park and the Wanderers are within a 10 minute drive). Surrounded by restaurants and shops the Rosebank Shopping Centre is just a short walk away. The hotel's two restaurants are both excellent – Fresh  and Butcher Block Grill – but our passion is reserved for the award-winning Circle Bar, definitely one of the places to be seen in the city. The Seven Colours Spa, a brand from Mauritius, is the first of its kind in South Africa and specializes in holistic treatments that re-energise and open up the chakras. The 318 state-of-the-art contemporary rooms include rainfor-est showers, i-pod docks and LCD TVs for comfort and convenience.

**Style 8, Atmosphere 7, Location 8**

**The Saxon** *(right)*
36 Saxon Road, Sandhurst
Tel: 011 292 6000
www.thesaxon.com
Rates: R6,400–25,600

The Saxon has been voted the World's Leading Boutique Hotel for the last six consecutive years. It might have somthing to do with the luxurious African elegance, it might be to do with the continued patronage of  numerous high profile guests from the continent and beyond. Like the Fairlawns (see page 42) it is situated in sprawling, lush gardens and exudes a sens of calm and tranquility perfect for slipping away from the sounds of the city. The design melds traditional African design and objets with modern luxury and convenience, while also concentrating on the minute attention to detail and the all important personal touches. The Saxon makes water a focal point, with the exterior centered on the spectacular infinity pool. The entrance exudes power, with its feature staircase sweeping around a huge glass dome allowing in the vast African sky. There is an emphasis on good food here, with a fine dining restaurant which pulls in the best of the local produce, a more infomal poolside bar and an intimate wine cellar for those who want their privacy. The spa offers a selection of hydrotherapies and a Rasul Chamber (mud and steam in one go) and some more alternative treatments including Sound and Colour therapies. With all modcons to boot, the Saxon is a serious contender for the city's most complete hotel.

**Style 10, Atmosphere 9, Location 10**

 **Southern Sun** *(left)*
**Hyde Park**
Hyde Park Shopping Centre,
1st Road, Hyde Park
Tel: 011 341 8080
www.southernsun.com
Rates: R1,431–1,537

The Southern Sun Hyde Park, opened at the end of September 2009 and is the only hotel in the upmarket Hyde

Park Shopping Centre. This shopping centre is home to some exceptional restaurants (Santorini and Willoughby & co – see Eat) and shops (Samsonite, L'Occitane, Max Mara – see Shop). The 132 stylish contemporary rooms offer panoramic views of the Sandton skyline. Although, the highlight is the roof top pool deck with an infinity pool and views stretching out over the northern suburbs and, of course, a pool bar for those in need of sundowners. There's even a gym up top for those who want a work out with a view, perfect for those with a slight deistic/narcissistic complex. The elegant Bice restaurant serves up equally elegant Italian cooking and the Daruma Sushi and Tempura bar does what it says on the tin.

**Style 8, Atmosphere 8, Location 8**

**Ten Bompas Hotel** *(right)*
10 Bompas Road, Dunkeld West
Tel: 011 325 2442
www.tenbompas.com
Rates: R3,500

Ten Bompas was originally a private home tucked down a road in one of Jo'burg's leafy suburbs. It has since been converted onto one of Jo'burg's most popular boutique hotels. The striking modern design, replete with long elegant curves and clean simple lines, is infused with contemporary African art and sculpture lining the walls of the balconies. The ten suites are simple, colourful and comfortable, with each being split into living room and bedroom; they all open up into the garden or onto a small balcony. Kitted out with a free mini-bar, steam bath and

a fireplace it is up to guests to inject their own brand of romance. One of the real selling points of Ten Bompas is the restaurant, Sides. In 2005 it was ranked in the top 10 in South Africa, something that might be to do with the impressive size of its cellar, home to almost 5,000 different wines.

**Style 7, Atmosphere 6, Location 6**

**Tintswalo Waterfall** *(top)*
Corner of R55 and Maxwell Drive, Midrand
Tel: 011 234 2456
www.tintswalo.co.za
Rates: R1,800

This is a gem of a property outside Jo'burg, although still within spitting distance of Sandton, with views over-looking polo fields and stretching out to the Magaliesberg Mountains beyond. The modern rustic design (it's basically a posh barn conversion) sits sympathetically within the landscape and is the perfect escape for those wanting to release some of the urban pressure. The decor is intentionally visceral juxtaposing roughly cut wood and stone with sleek modern furniture and all necessary creature comforts. The Feedroom (yes, it's continuing the rustic farm theme) delivers farm-fresh ingredients to diners in an all encom-passing international menu (still hard to escape even out here). For those needing to unwind they can walk the hotel's own trails or try and relax at the Vital Source Spa, which offers a variety of treatments as well as the run-of-the-mill gym, sauna and steam bath.

**Style 8, Atmosphere 8, Location 6**

**The Westcliff** *(bottom)*
67 Jan Smuts Avenue, Westcliff
Tel: 011 481 6000
www.westcliff.co.za
Rates: R3,000

The Westcliff is Jo'burg's most iconic hotel. Perched on the side of a hill, only half an hour's drive from the airport, the Westcliff offers spectacu-lar views of the city's leafy suburbs. The 80 rooms and 35 suites are all elegantly decorated in a classic post-colonial style with most capitalizing on the hotel's position. The theme continues with the expansive views from the La Belle Terrasse restaurant – offering well-presented and delicious international cooking. Inside, the Polo Bar, reminiscent of an old fashioned Gentleman's club, has a vibrant cock-tail scene and is popular with the city's movers and shakers; although for those who want their sundowners al fresco the pool deck is perfect. Equipped for both the business traveller (WiFi, con-ference and business centre) and those in search of a little light relaxation (two swimming pools and a floodlit tennis court), as well as a Botanica Spa for some serious pampering, the Westcliff is the perfect Jo'burg hideaway.

**Style 8, Atmosphere 8, Location 8**

# eat...

Jozis (the Jo'burg natives) are social animals who love to eat, drink and, above all, be merry. Widely considered the friendliest city-based bunch in the country, Jozis navigate their way through the urban landscape to suss out the city's many restaurants and cafés. Naturally, we've followed their lead and bring you reviews of the best, right here on these hallowed, gorgeously glossy pages.

As a melting pot of cultures – including African, European, Asian and South American – South African cuisine is as diverse and as cosmopolitan as you'd expect. With the exception of the legendary *braai* (a South African barbecue that's become a rite of passage for men), the choices at Jo'burg restaurants are varied to say the least. Traditional cooking includes *bobotie* (spiced mince with an egg topping), potjie (stew) and piled-high meat, *biltong* (cured meat), *boerewors* (sausage), and, of course, steak cut from anything that breathes (from beef right through to zebra). Modern South African cooking, however, builds on the basic principles of traditional cuisine and adds a fabulous fusion of international influences that makes for truly lipsmacking fare.

Unfortunately, the majority of Jozis do not have the financial means to explore beyond the basic foodstuffs of maize and chicken. For a taste of traditional treats, it would be worth organising a culinary tour out to Soweto; visitors can expect to

sample *skop* (sheep's brain) and humorously named *walki talkies* (chicken's feet and head). Thankfully, those arriving in Jo'burg with a reasonable budget can skip such, er, delicacies and head straight for the gourmet kitchen.

Those more comfortable with European fare can still get their grubby little mitts on French, Greek, Portuguese, Lebanese, Indian and Japanese cuisine. Steaks are big business in Jo'burg, too, and lovers of red meat certainly won't go hungry. Good cuts and big slabs of the bloody stuff are generally affordable, and are served in the majority of mainstream restaurants.

In short, Jo'burg is a city of constant change. This not only applies to the people and the culture, but also to the ever-changing culinary landscape. Armed with your appetite and a sense of adventure, you can't go far wrong.

Due to space restrictions, a number of excellent eateries didn't make it into this guide – but we highly recommend Villamore for fabulous fish, Auberge St Michelle for fantastic French and Yamato for super sushi.

Roots

# the best restaurants

**Top ten:**
1. Roots
2. Mosaic
3. Thomas Maxwell
4. The Saxon
5. Ghazal – Bryanston
6. Assaggi
7. Fishmonger
8. Grill House – Rosebank
9. Wang Thai
10. The Attic

**Food:**
1. Roots
2. Mosaic
3. Thomas Maxwell
4. Wombles
5. Fishmonger

**Service:**
1. Mosaic
2. The Saxon
3. Thomas Maxwell
4. Wombles
5. The Attic

**Atmosphere:**
1. Thomas Maxwell
2. Wombles
3. Mosaic
4. The Grillhouse
5. The Attic

**Angies** *(left)*
39 Pierre Road, Roodepoort,
Honeydew
Tel: 082 5543 359
www.angiesrestaurant.co.za
Open: 9am–late Wed–Sun
**International**                    **R180**

Over 10 years old, this rustic retreat is situated in the quiet valley of Honeydew (about 40 minutes from Sandton) and offers its patrons an intimate dining experience beside a roaring open fireplace. On hot summer evenings the restaurant throws open the doors to a number of sun-drenched patios, with plenty of drooping trees to offer shade to those supping. The menu comprises comfort food classics for when there's a chill in the air, including braised oxtail, duck and cherry pie and warm chocolate mousse. For warmer days a selection of salads and wraps make for light bites indeed. Described as 'family-friendly', the restaurant also offers stressed-out parents respite from their demanding offspring with a dedicated children's play area and organised pony rides every Sunday. Retired types may want to steer clear.

**Food 8, Service 7, Atmosphere 7**

**Assaggi** *(right)*
Post Office Centre, 30 Rudd Rd,
Illovo, Sandton
Tel: 011 268 1370
Open: noon–2pm, 6.30–9pm.
Closed Sundays and Monday lunch.
**Italian**                    **R 250**

Assaggi (meaning taste) is Italian in every sense of the word, with Luciana, the current chef, taking over from her son in 2002. By ensuring it remains a family-run affair, the restaurant wouldn't look out of place in an Italian city, although, rather surprisingly, it is found in one of Jo'burg's shopping centres. The atmosphere is unpretentious and casual, with unfussy décor that includes crisp white tablecloths and beech-wood chairs for an uncluttered aesthetic. Diners can expect frenetic Italian energy to unfold all around them, especially when Luciana is on the prowl, taking orders, barking at staff and running about the place with piled-high plates of food. You could, of course, try to soften her up with a few choice words in Italian – something she welcomes and will engender instant fondness. The simple menu comprises all the usual Italian staples, using only the freshest ingredients and offering up a slice of homemade goodness to its pasta-loving patrons.

**Food 9, Service 8, Atmosphere 8**

**The Attic** *(bottom)*
24 4th Avenue, Parkhurst
Tel: 011 880 6102
Open: 6–10pm Mon; noon–3pm &
6.30–10pm Tues–Sun
**Fusion**                    **R140**

The Attic serves up excellent food in a wonderfully casual environment. The rustic-chic interior is filled with solid wooden tables of varying sizes and shapes alongside a mismatch of antique chairs, making for an eclectic space. Old photos, paintings and knick-knacks adorn the walls, while huge antique gilded mirrors reflect beaded chandeliers and exposed rafters. When it comes to the menu, the

THE Attic

THE Attic 011 880 6102

chef/owner is fanatical about sourcing the very best produce; wherever possible, he ensures everything that goes into his dishes is organic, free-range and sustainable. The menu also changes with the seasons to make the best of fresh ingredients, and attempts to pair wine and beer with different dishes to bring out the flavour of both the food and wine. A must-try is The Attic's signature Mozambican crab fettuccine with coriander, chilli and lime – a to-dine-for dish if ever there was one! Despite both indoor and al fresco seating, booking here is still essential.

**Food 9, Service 9, Atmosphere 9**

**The Baron Sandown** *(left)*
Shop 11, 24 Central, Corner of Gwen Lane and Fredman Drive, Sandown
Tel: 011 883 8435/6
www.thebaron.co.za
Open: daily, noon–10.30pm
**Contemporary** R220

Set in the heart of the Sandton business district, this is one of the most vibrant restaurants you are ever likely to stumble across. Loved by sharp-suited local bankers, a largely business crowd congregates in the restaurant's rotating booths to down drinks and bitch about fellow colleagues long after office hours. Be sure to book if you want a booth – they get pretty crammed. Food-wise, the menu's plethora of

meat dishes are particularly good and are cooked to perfection – there are, however, a number of other fish, poultry and vegetarian dishes should you prefer less machismo with your meal. Don't be put off by the fact that this is a franchise, either – it's pretty damn fabulous.

**Food 9, Service 7, Atmosphere 9**

**Beirut** *(right)*
11th street, Parkmore, Sandton
Tel: 011 884 1015
Open: daily, noon–late
**Middle Eastern** **R140**

This unassuming restaurant has grown from a tiny fast food joint to a full-blown catering service. Its two venues serve arguably the best Lebanse food in Jo'burg, and with prime position beside the road patrons can either sit inside or on the pavement to watch the world go by. Those in a rush should order the lamb *schwarma* – the juicy meat is full of flavour and will give you energy while on-the-go. The fried haloumi and vine leaf *dolmades* make great starters, while the *tabbouleh* and *kibbi* are for the more adventurous. Wash everything down with Lebanese beer or wine, and enjoy the belly dancers that pass through to perform at the weekends.

**Food 8, Service 7, Atmosphere 8.**

**Casalinga** *(top-right)*
Rocky Ridge Road, Off Beyers
Naudé Drive, Muldersdrift
Tel: 087 941 1223
www.casalinga.co.za
Open: noon–3pm, 6–10pm Weds–Sun
**Italian**                              **R220**

Found 40 minutes outside of Sandton, Casalinga is a bit of a trek but a
worthwhile one nevertheless. Once
the private home of the De Lucas, the
couple made the decision to open it
up in the late 80s and haven't looked
back since. For 20 odd years this venue
has been serving its roster of regulars,
offering wonderful Italian dishes amid
rustic furnishings. It has been a popular
venue for weddings, and with an intimate, somewhat romantic setting it's
not hard to see why. The wine cellar

offers a vast selection for those plan-
ning on getting merry – customers can
even go on a tour, picking out bottles
that match their particular occasion
– while the expansive gardens provide
the perfect setting for an after-dinner
smooch under the stars.

**Food 7, Service 8, Atmosphere 7**

**Col' Cacchio** *(bottom-right)*
Benmore Gardens Shopping
Centre, Upper Level, Sandton
Tel: 011 783 7650
www.colcacchio.co.za
Open: noon–10pm. Closed Sundays.
**Italian Pizza/Pasta**           **R130**

Sometimes it's the simple things in life
that bring the most pleasure, and such

is the case with pizza – an easy-peasy recipe of cheese, tomato and ham on a thin crust can bring a smile to even the most discerning foodie's face. Italian chain Col' Cacchio serves up some of the most perfect pizzas in town, and has a branch conveniently located within the Benmore Shopping Centre for easy refuelling between shops. Pastas and salads add to the already-bulging menu, while a vast variety of pizza toppings makes choosing just one extremely difficult. Fortunately diners don't have to, but can mix and match at leisure. Complete with ample seating both inside and out, this is causal Italian food at its quickest and best.

**Food 8, Service 8, Atmosphere 8**

**Espresso Caffe** *(right)*
Shop 23, 4th Avenue, Parkhurst
Tel: 011 447 8700
Open 8am–10pm (8pm Sun).
Closed Mondays.
**Mediterranean** **R130**

Espresso Caffe, a family-run Mediterranean eatery, opened over a decade ago and has become something of a local institution. Winning over its chic clientele with consistently good food and the highest possible standard of service, the casual café is the perfect place to enjoy a languid lunch or sumptuous supper. Found on an extended pavement on 4th Avenue, the restaurant is pretty much an outdoors experience – there is space inside but nobody ever uses it. The extensive menu caters for most tastes with pizzas, pastas,

65

meat, fish and salad dishes all available in both large or mezze-style portions. There's also something of a cocktail culture here, with after-work drinks being taken by those with offices close by. Please note that your plastic's no good here – cold, hard cash only.

**Food 8, Service 8, Atmosphere 8**

**Faff** *(bottom-right)*
44 The Avenue, Norwood
Tel 011 728 2434  www.faff.co.za
Open: 12.30–3pm, 6–10pm Tues–Fri;
7.30–11pm Sat; noon–9pm Sun
**Global eclectic**          **R195**

Sometimes it is really quite tricky to effectively categorize the cooking of a restaurant and Faff is just one of these. Incorporating everything form crispy duck pancakes to sashimi, ceviche, Schnitzel, osso bucco and nasi goring if is nigh on impossible to classify – but then again that's maybe what ex-travelling shoe salesman turned restaurateur Dave Wallace intended. The bright, simple dining room is elegant and uncluttered with colourful, modern fruit and vegetable-inspired paintings on the wall, while floor to ceiling windows flood the space with natural light. For those who want their thinking done for them the selection of degustation (tasting) menus cuts down the decision-making, or faff, factor. A well thought out global wine list compliments the cooking and picks up vintages from as far afield as Israel and Chile; or, for those preferring spirits, a decent cocktail list is available.

ing, with a black and white theme furnished by comfortable benches, flowers on tables and a 16-seat tapas and cocktail bar. The menu is a heady mix of Spanish and Mediterranean classics, and ranges from cold tapas (*tortilla*, *boquerones* and *albondigas*) to more Mediterranean-inspired plates (haloumi, crostini and steak tartare). We recommend sticking to the tapas selection to get the best out of Fino.

**Food 7, Service 8, Atmosphere 8**

**Fishmonger** *(top-middle)*
Thrupps Centre,
204 Oxford Road, Illovo
Tel: 011 268 0067/8
Open: daily, noon–3.30pm, 6–9.30pm
**Seafood                    R300**

If you prefer fresh to frozen, then Fishmonger is the place to salivate over seafood in Jo'burg. Run by its owner, the landmark restaurant in Illovo offers seafood and service in equal measures across a neat indoor/outdoor space, with much of its fish only caught just the day before. Booking is essential as diners flock here in their droves, and the bustling crowd keep the atmosphere relaxed and free of any pretentious airs. The menu includes everything from Scottish salmon, Falkland calamari, sardines, black mussels, seafood *espetada* and sushi. Prawns, of course, are a house speciality and come in all plump shapes and sizes, while the healthy Greek salad with squid heads and lobster bisque make for a delicious starter.

**Food 9, Service 8, Atmosphere 8**

**Food 8, Service 8, Atmosphere 7**

**Fino** *(left)*
19 4th Avenue, off 7th Avenue, Parktown North
Tel: 011 447 4608 www.finojhb.co.za
Open: noon–3pm, 6–10.30pm. Closed Monday lunches.
**Spanish/European            R210**

Fino is the best Spanish restaurant in Jo'burg – not that there's much competition, mind – and is perfectly poised on a quiet street in Parktown North. This charming little eatery is easily identified by the white decking outside, which provides a great platform for long summer evenings with a glass of wine in-hand and a plate or three of tapas. The interior is simple but charm-

### Ghazal                                    *(right)*
Coachman's Crossing, Peter Place, Bryanston
Tel: 011 706 9826
www.ghazal.co.za
Open: daily, noon–11pm
**North Indian**                        **R170**

Ghazal – deriving from the art of ancient Indian love poetry – is located in the quiet shopping centre of Peter Place in the middle of Sandton, and is quite possibly the best Indian restaurant in all of Jo'burg. The menu focuses on classic dishes from Northern India, and will impress even the most discerning curry fiend with fabulous favourites that range from hot to bloody scorching. The interior is unlike any other curry house you will have come across, with huge windows looking out over the suburbs, paved stone floors and large industrial lights hanging from the ceiling. This is more New York than New Delhi. For those unable to get a table, or simply too lazy to leave the hotel, they do offer a take-away service, delivered direct to your room.

**Food 9, Service 7, Atmosphere 7**

### Gramadoelas                              *(left)*
Market Theatre, Newtown
Tel: 011 838 6960
www.gramadoelas.co.za
Open: noon–11.30pm Tues–Sat; 6–11.30pm Mon
**South African**                       **R210**

Established in 1967, Gramadoelas has moved from a basement garage in Hillbrow (now Jo'burg's slum) to the Market Theatre in Newtown. Having started life as an essay in inclusion (diners of all colours, backgrounds and financial means were welcomed) it has carved out a niche in the city's affections. If its reservations book is good enough for a roster of presidents, actors and royal family members, then it's certainly good enough for you. Today the menu encompasses true South African fare, with a range of slightly more exotic dishes ranging from mopani worms and crocodile steak to ostrich, and is widely considered one of the best South African restaurants in the country. The décor here is styulish but busy, with little knick-knacks, artefacts and mirrors making for a warm, intimate atmosphere.

**Food 8, Service 8, Atmosphere 8**

### The Grillhouse                          *(bottom)*
Shop 70, The Firs Hyatt Centre, Oxford Road, Rosebank
Tel: 011 880 3945
www.thegrill.co.za
Open: daily, noon–2.30pm, 6.30–11pm. Closed Saturday lunch.
**Steak**                                **R200**

The Grillhouse is one of South Africa's longest surviving steakhouses, and boy does it show. Offering its discerning diners mouthwatering meals within cool club-esque interiors, you'd never guess that it was slap-bang in the middle of a busy shopping centre – had you not walked through to get to it, that is. Fabulous steaks and ribs go hand-in-hand with fish, chicken and vegetarian dishes, while the excellent wines and malts are brought up from the well-stocked wine cellar to quench the thirst of parched patrons. The décor itself is sophisticated and stylish (and kind of

New York), surprising indeed for such a traditional steakhouse, with leather booths, dark wood, low-lighting and exposed brickwork. Those who don't want to join the carnivores in the dining room can prop up the handcrafted bar or party in the private dining room, which has enough space to swing 70 guests. When you've finished at The Grillhouse, mooch over to Katzy's next door and take in a spot of live jazz.

**Food 9, Service 8, Atmosphere 9**

---

### La Belle Terrasse *(left)* at The Westcliff

The Westcliff Hotel, 67 Jan Smuts Avenue, Parktown
Tel: 011 481 6000
www.westcliff.co.za
Open: daily, 7–10am, 7–10pm; 11.30am–3pm Sunday brunch.
**International**            **R350**

As The Westcliff hotel's signature restaurant, its well-heeled guests have great expectations for La Belle Terrasse – and fortunately they are more than fulfilled here. The restaurant sits overlooking the lushness of the northern suburbs and on a warm summer's evening dinner is taken on the expansive terrace, where the cooking seems worthy of a Michelin-star. Whether it's a beautiful breakfast or a decadent dinner, La Belle Terrasse's international menu will cater to even the most discerning diner's palate. The dishes offer a complex, but not overly extravagant, melding of tastes, with more than a passing nod to the East. Sunday brunches are legendary, with all-inclusive buffets offering platters piled-high with sushi, salads and meats, as well as divine desserts. Booking is essential – so make sure you save yourself a seat.

**Food 8, Service 8, Atmosphere 9**

---

### Louis XVI *(middle)*

160 Jan Smuts Avenue, Rosebank

Tel: 011 447 6244  www.louisxvi.co.za
Open: 7.30–11pm (11.30pm Thurs–
Sat). Closed Sundays and Mondays.
**French**                          **R230**

The stylish interior of Louis XVI has
all the hallmarks of extravagant 18th-
century Paris; ornate gilded mirrors,
Baccarat chandeliers, and a rich bur-
gundy velvet covering the banquettes
and offsetting the stark whiteness of
the neatly pressed linens. Part-Marie
Antoinette and part-exclusive bordello
the interior has the makings of some
very decadent goings on. Aside from
the spectacular splendour of its Ver-
sace-esque interiors, Louis XVI owes
its reputation to executive chef Bruno
Beurel. Originally hailing from Alsace
and then working his way through Paris
the Frenchness of his cooking and the
influences they bring are immediately
apparent. Many of the old favourites
are trotted out from *pâte de foie gras*
and French onion soup to *coq au vin*
and *confit de canard*. However, as is often the case, the best is saved until last

with overly indulgent and decadently
rich puddings including Jo'burg's best-
*crème brûlée* and the theatrical *crêpes
Suzette*. Bruno has also imported a selection of his favourite French cheeses
to finish things off with an odorous
flourish. All of these are complimented
by some of France and South Africa's
top wines under the knowledgeable
stewardship of the wait staff.

**Food 9, Service 8, Atmosphere 9**

.............................................................

**Mezepoli**                        *(right)*
Shop SL 26, Melrose Piazza,
Melrose Arch, Whitley Rd,
Melrose North
Tel: 011 684 1162
www.mezepoli.co.za
Open: daily, noon–late
**Meze**                            **R230**

Set in the Melrose Arch complex, this
restaurant is a sibling to modern Greek
taverna Plaka (see page 73) and overlooks the piazza in Melrose Arch's high

end and expansive shopping centre, for an interesting essay in people watching. Specialising in mezze-style dishes, diners can indulge on a little of everything from a wide range of Greek to Spanish mini tapas-style portions. Middle-Eastern classics also feature on the menu, as does delectable dim sum. Mezepoli offers quick and filling urban dining in a stylish setting. Given its location many see it as the perfect place to cut loose at the end of a busy working day or simply pick up some sustenance on mid-shopping or a waistline-watching lunch for those ladies who do it so well. With the clean, no-nonsense décor and a hip clientele, Mezepoli is deserving of its crowds.

**Food 8, Service 8, Atmosphere 8**

## Mosaic *(right)*
The Orient Hotel, Francolin Conservation Area, Crocodile River Valley, Elandsfontein
Tel: 012 371 2902
www.restaurantmosaic.com
Open: 7–10am, noon–3pm, 7–9pm Weds–Sat
**International**                          **R245**

Having recently been awarded the accolade of the best restaurant in South Africa, Mosaic is definitely worth a visit. Set in the spectacular Orient Hotel 40 minutes out of Sandton the décor and gastronomy can only be described as sensational. Working from a basic international palate the cooking has been influenced from India, Morocco, Turkey and the Middle East drawing in subtle fusions while making most of the fresh and organic locally-sourced ingredients. The décor picks up the look and

feel of the hotel and the food, drawing inspiration from the Silk Route, North Africa and the sub-continent, and pays attention to all the right details. The food is based around degustation tasting menus – ranging from five courses to the seven-course Grande Degustation with or without wine pairings. The food certainly isn't cheap, with the entry level two-course a la carte coming in at R245, but definitely worth it.

**Food 9, Service 9, Atmosphere 9**

**Moyo** *(left)*
Melrose Arch, Shop no 5 The High Street, Melrose Arch, Melrose
Tel: 011 684 1477 www.moyo.co.za
Open: daily, 11am–11pm
**African**                                    **R240**

This African experience restaurant, set in the stylish Melrose Arch shopping centre, is far less kitsch and more stylish than you might expect. Inside, its interiors are a chaotic celebration of all things African and look to span the continent in look and feel, ranging from a North African style tent to a seemingly carved out cave. However, the terrace on a warm evening can't really be beaten. The menu follows the theme of the interior drawing in dishes from Morocco, Nigeria, Senegal, Mozambique and, of course, South Africa. Defintiely pandering to the 'experience' diner guests are greeted by 'Wishy-Washy' ladies who introduce them to the age-old tradition of African hand-washing and face-painting; it's all slightly gimmicky, but hey you're on holiday so relax. Live music and performances sometimes accompany dinner to complete the authenticity of the African evening.

*eat...*

**Food 8, Service 7, Atmosphere 8**

.........................................................................

▮ **Plaka** *(left)*
▮ Illovo Centre,
Oxford Road, Illovo
Tel: 011 268 1338 www.plaka.co.za
Open: daily, 11am–11pm
**Greek**                                    **R200**

Plaka has worked hard for its good name, with mouthwatering Greek cooking and a lively Mediterranean atmosphere to match. Set within cool contemporary interiors, complete with soothing blues and turquoises, this establishment specialises in meze and wine (and as anyone mad about the Med will know, these are best enjoyed together). Highly recommend is

the *souvlaki*, made of succulent grilled cubes of beef or chicken on a skewer. It's a great shame that all of the above is enjoyed in a busy shopping centre, which may put potential patrons off, but the noise from the busy precinct doesn't carry through.

**Food 8, Service 8, Atmosphere 8**

.........................................................................

▮ **Rocket** *(middle)*
▮ 362 Rivonia Boulevard,
Corner of 11th Avenue, Rivonia
Tel: 011 234 8807
www.rocketrestaurant.co.za
Open: daily, 11am–2am
**Contemporary**                          **R160**

Bar-cum-restaurant Rivonia is renowned for its food and booze, and

is a great spot to watch the comings and goings of the local neighbourhood. Predominantly the preserve of suits after work, Rocket is all about light, breezy interiors with cream walls, polished wooden floors and al fresco decking. Its simplicity is reflected in the menu, too, with sandwiches, pastas and light snacks making up most of its offerings, together with a range of heartier mains for the truly hungry. Highly recommended are the rostis, to be enjoyed between gulps of a house cocktail. On the off chance you have to wait for a table, grab a stool at the Shooter Bar and order a beer or three.

**Food 8, Service 8, Atmosphere 8**

### Roots *(right)*
Letamo Game Estate, Barlett Road (off Ventersdorp Road), Krugersdorp
Tel: 011 668 7000
www.forumhomini.co.za
Open: daily, noon–3pm, 7–10pm
**French Fusion**                    **R180**

Found a 40-minute drive north of Jo'burg, Roots is part of the Forum Homini Boutique Hotel (see Sleep) and is set in the Cradle of Humankind (an UNESCO site). The restaurant itself has been winning awards ever since chef Philippe Wagenfuhrer took over the reins with a host of accolades under its ever-expanding belt. The menu uses rich, visceral ingredients reminiscent of the history that surrounds the area – marrowbone, game, roots,

plants and fruit – and then gives them a neat 21st-century twist. Wagenfuhrer believes in pairing his cooking with suitable wines and has developed an interesting set of rules to play by. Although quite a slog out of town, Roots is well worth the visit but we recommend you stay the night to take full advantage of the wine list.

**Food 9, Service 8, Atmosphere 9**

**The Saxon**                    *(right)*
**Restaurant**
36 Saxon Road, Sandhurst,
Tel: 011 292 6000   www.thesaxon.com
Open: daily, 7am–12.30pm, 7–10pm
**African**                        **R375**

Found within the beautiful boutique hotel of the same name, The Saxon restaurant really redefines the meaning of fine dining. Set in super-stylish surroundings, the interiors are minimal, modern and understated – leaving the focus on the food, as indeed it should be. Crisp white-clothed tables set the scene for the mouthwatering menu, with head chef Rudi Liebenberg using only the freshest local ingredients to concoct a fabulous fusion of African- and Mediterranean-inspired dishes. The breakfast buffet is the restaurant's signature, however, with a showstopping spread of fruit, season berries, homemade compotes and coulis laid out for wide eyes and big bellies. For those wanting a little extra intimacy then they should book into the enchanting wine cellar where they can really get to grips with the wine list.

**Food 9, Service 9, Atmosphere 9**

**Thomas Maxwell**              *(top)*
140 11th Street,
Parkmore, Sandton
Tel: 011 784 1575
www.thomasmaxwell.co.za
Open: noon–2.30pm, 6–9.30pm
Mon–Fri; 6–9.30pm Sat
**Eclectic**                       **R220**

Thomas Maxwell's 'New York-style' bistro is one of our favourite restaurants in town. Based in Parkmore in Sandton, the eclectic menu – which ranges from mussels and chips to warthog carpaccio – rarely changes thanks to a local loyal following. What used to be the best-kept secret in Jo'burg has now found wider appeal with diners-flocking in their droves, but don't let them put you off. Don't let the fairly unassuming entrance deter you, either – once you get inside you'll be greeted with chic exposed brick walls and vintage furniture. Thomas, the owner and chef, is passionate about food and cites Brit offal aficionado Fergus Henderson among his influences. His love of wine also shines through and is reflected in the extensive and international wine list. The food is so damn good that you might find it a little tricky to squeeze in their amazing complimentary cupcakes at the end of the meal.

**Food 9, Service 9, Atmosphere 9**

**Turn 'n' Tender**             *(left)*
Corner of 3rd Avenue and 7th Avenue, Parktown North
Tel: 011 788 7933
www.turnntender.co.za
Open: daily, 11.30am–10.30pm (9pm Sun)
**Steak**                          **R230**

Turn 'n' Tender has been around for a while, well into its fourth decade of operation this small and well regarded steak house has become a Jo'burg instituion. Meat-lovers flock here in their carnivorous droves to sample melt-in-your-mouth steaks. In fact pretty much everything on the menu has been cut from some animal or other, so vegetarians might need to look elsewhere. Know-it-all waiters are on-hand to advise novices on the different cuts of meat and the best wines to match them. The simple interior is rather basic, with dark wooden tables and chairs, concrete flooring and orange-hued light emitting from the cylindrical shades that dangle overhead. If you're looking for something a little more romantic or quaint, Turn 'n' Tender has a sister restaurant called The Mini Tender Steak Boutique in nearby Emmarentia.

**Food 8, Service 9, Atmosphere 9**

**Wang Thai** *(top)*
1st Floor, Nelson Mandela Square, Sandton City
Tel: 011 784 8484 www.wangthai.co.za
Open: daily, noon–2.30pm, 6–10.30pm
**Thai**                              **R200**

Wang Thai is slightly unusual in that it offers diners some really well-crafted Thai food in South Africa, a country not usually known for its Thai restaurants. Drawing from experiences back home guests are treated to the levels of hospitality usually only experienced in Thailand, with deliciously spicy cooking and razor-sharp service served up in equal measures. All dishes here are prepared by a Thai masterchef who sources all the necessary ingredients directly from his suppliers in Thailand; the result is a menu that takes diners on a culinary tour through flavours that are sweet, sour, spicy and subtle. Come as a group, select a spread of dishes and share them around to make the most of Wang Thai's offerings. If you sit close enough you can catch all the behind-the-scenes action via a big glass window that looks into the kitchen. Voyeurism and fabulous food – what more could you want?

**Food 9, Service 8, Atmosphere 8**

**Wombles** *(bottom)*
17 3rd Avenue, Parktown North
Tel: 011 880 2470 www.wombles.co.za
Open: noon–2.30pm, 6–9.30pm Mon–Fri; 6–9.30pm Sat
**Steaks**                            **R170**

Situated in a meticulously renovated house in the up-market suburb of Parktown North, Wombles is all about homely glamour with antique wooden furniture and contemporary furnishings making for an interesting and eclectic interior. Large wine glasses and silver cutlery grace the tables all underneath blood red walls. Famed for its reasonably priced and oh-so tender steaks, the menu is presided over by Rhodesian owner/chef Duncan Barker. Concessions are made for those who are spurn red meat with a decent selection of poultry and fish. Wombles is great all year round, but possibly best enjoyed in the summer when spacious verandas beckon for boozy lunches in the afternoons or romantic dinners in the evenings. During the winter months the restaurant turns from chic to cosy, with both outside and inside fires to warm up chilly patrons.

**Food 9, Service 9, Atmosphere 9**

# drink...

Often referred to as the Los Angeles of South Africa – with almost as much silicone but not quite as many superstars – it's hardly surprising that Jo'burg's drinking dens are, on the whole, pretty damn stylish. Perhaps such effort is made with its bar scene in response to the criticism from other South African cities that Jo'burg lacks style? Whatever it is, Jo'burg certainly knows how to provide buzzing bars for its boozehounds, from the sleek venues found in its hotels to the outlandish outposts down its sidestreets. The party's pumping here, and there's no denying that Jozis know how to drink, dance and have a bloody good time.

One of the biggest grievances visitors have with Jo'burg's bars are their closing times; in short, their doors shut far too early, particularly for party animals looking to carry on with hedonistic pursuits long into the night. Many establishments shut up shop between midnight and 2am at the weekends, while it's an even earlier time of 10pm during the week. Thankfully, hotel bars stay open longer for residents looking to have their fill of their liquor cabinet – and let's face it, who isn't? Unlike Europeans who eat late and drink even later, Jozis hit the bars straight after work, book restaurant reservations for seven or eight, and call in at a few more bars immediately after to get home in plenty of time for bed. Clubs are usually reserved for the weekend.

That said, South Africans have developed notoriety for drinking and driving; a bone of contention among locals if ever there was one, as there is a poor infrastructure of taxis and late-night public transport available other than pre-booking at hotels. That's no excuse, though, so make sure you don't drive over the limit – two beers, in case you're wondering. Arrange a taxi before you head out so you can enjoy your evening without worrying how you're getting back to the hotel – or whether you'll make it back at all.

Drinking at hotel bars is a costly affair, but is reflective of its clientele. Expect to pay between R20-35 for a local beer – a price, no doubt, locals would flinch at. The city's elite, however, flock to hotel bars in their fashionable droves for a slice of something stylish; consider the award-winning Circle Bar at The Rosebank Hotel or the Polo Lounge at The Westcliff Hotel. For many locals stand-alone bars are a cheaper alternative, and, in many cases, more conveniently located. Expect to pay between R12–20 for a local beer. Naturally, Jo'burg has much-loved landmarks that cater to all; why not try the Radium Beerhall, the oldest bar in Jo'burg, or the Jolly Rodger, a quintessential English pub.

Whether you prefer hotel bars or stand-alone establishments, make sure you explore beyond the confines of your hotel. Jo'burg offers up somewhere to suit every aesthetic and musical taste, so work your way through our recommendations below to find your personal favourite.

drink...

Melrose Arch Pool Bar

### The Attic                    *(left)*

24 4th Avenue, Corner of 10th Street and 4th Avenue, Parkhurst
Tel: 011 880 6102
Open: 6pm–10pm Mon; noon–3pm, 6.30–10pm Tues–Sun

Featured in our Eat section – and for good reason – The Attic is an equally good place to come for liquid sustenance as it is for its gorgeous grub. It's amazing just how many people you can cram into the small, unassuming bar attached to the restaurant – then just watch them jostle for dancing space! Once the chef has finished up in the kitchen it's off with the overalls and into the bar to spin tunes and pour drinks for the party-loving crowd. Whether downing shots or sidling up against a sexy stranger on the dance floor, The Attic proves that bars within restaurants can sometimes be better than a full-on club. Come smart or casual – anything goes.

### The Baron Sandown      *(right)*

Shop 11, 24 Central, Corner of Gwen Lane and Fredman Drive, Sandown
Tel: 011 883 8435/6
www.thebaron.co.za
Open: daily, noon–10.30pm

The Baron Sandown is another after-work favourite frequented by sharp-suited business execs. Friday is buzzing, with the mature crowd using liquid psychology to ease the stresses and strains of office life. Prop up the bar inside or sit outside in the courtyard for the best people-watching opportunities in the venue. Those wanting to soak up the booze can order snacks from the bars – highly recommended is the bar platter – with the chirpy bar staff catering to your every whim. Expect things to get a little wild here after tough – or particularly successful – trading weeks. Come on bonus day to watch things really spiral out of control.

### The Circle Bar at      *(bottom)*
### The Rosebank Hotel

Corner Tyrwhitt & Sturdee Avenues, Rosebank
Tel: 011 448 3600
www.therosebank.co.za
Open: daily, 11am–2am

Accolades and awards have been thrown at the recently refurbished Circle Bar, and it's not hard to see why. As the on-site watering hole at the prestigious Rosebank Hotel, the property's well-heeled guests expect nothing less than excellence. And that's exactly what they get here, with plush leather seats, colour-changing pods and subdued lighting. Highly recommended on the extensive cocktail menu is the signature Kiss Kiss Bang Bang, served with complimentary biltong on a silver platter. The drinks certainly aren't cheap, but at least you know what you're paying for here; a sexy surroundings and a sexy clientele more than make up for the hole in your pocket.

### Espresso Caffe    *(top)*
Shop 23, 4th Avenue, Parkhurst
Tel: 011 447 8700
Open 8am–10pm (8pm Sun).
Closed Mondays.

Despite being more café than bar – hence its name – Espresso Caffe is still a cool place to swig a bottle of ice-cold beer or two. With its position on an extended pavement making for a really relaxed and casual atmosphere, the café al fresco experience really strikes a chord with those wanting to grab a drink in the sunshine or make the most of the warm evenings under the twinkling stars. Sunday afternoons are particularly enjoyable, especially when a sporting event is being shown live on TV and the locals gather round to watch their beloved Boks being whipped by those damn Brits yet again. Breakfast, lunch and dinner menus are also available for those looking to line their stomachs.

### Fino    *(middle)*
Corner of 4th Avenue and 7th Avenue, Parktown North
Tel: 011 447 4608
www.finojhb.co.za
Open: noon–3pm, 6–10.30pm. Closed Sunday evenings and Monday lunch.

Situated in the leafy suburb of Parktown North, Fino is characterised by superb Spanish cooking and the blinding white decking outside. Though not necessarily a bar, it is certainly a stylish setting for a sangria or three under the warm evening sun. Perfect for a pre-dinner drink – outside in the summer, or inside at the mosaic bar in the winter – Fino caters to any discerning drinker's needs. For those who get a little peckish Fino's delectable variation on tapas, ranging from Mediterranean-style dishes to typically Spanish classics, are perfect for soaking up the booze. Drink, eat and truly indulge in chic but casual surroundings.

### Giles    *(bottom)*
9 Grafton Avenue, Craighall Park
Tel: 011 442 4056
Open: daily, 12.15–4pm, 6.15–10.30pm; 12.30–2.30pm Sun

*drink...*

Having been open for over 10 years, Giles – named after the famous cartoon strip – attracts a loyal following of locals who come mainly for after-work drinks and chit-chat at the bar. The interiors are festooned with comic strips, as is appropriate, and make for amusing reading when you've had one too many to engage in actual conversation. For a quick food fix order a plate of biltong at the bar, always manned unnervingly enthusiastic bartenders. Crowds tend to congregate here for the sporting fixtures shown on the TVs, with people spilling out on the street drinks still in-hand. Aside from the buzzing bar, the restaurant is a good spot for dinner with highly attentive waiters and an Anglo-French menu; highly recommended is the granny burger, fish and chips or Kudu pie.

### The Hyde Park Hotel Bar *(top-left)*

Hyde Park Shopping Centre, 1st Road, Hyde Park
Tel: 011 341 8080
www.southernsun.com
Open: daily, 11am–midnight

Set high above Hyde Park Shopping centre in the Southern Sun hotel, the Hyde Park Hotel bar is a brilliant place to prop up and admire the setting sun from afar. Complete with a large lounge area and dedicated cigar bar, it's no wonder hotel guests spend more time here than they do in their rooms. The bar overlooks the pool, too, meaning you can take your drink outside, settle yourself on a sunlounger and observe the toned bodies soaking up the rays or cooling off in the turquoise water. The bar itself offers a heavenly selection of whisky to savour, taste or simply shoot, and a number of rarer spirits that are otherwise hard to find in Jo'burg. The hotel's Italian restaurant, Bice Ristorante, finishes things off nicely before bed.

### Jolly Cool *(bottom-left)*

Corner of Fourth Avenue & Sixth Street, Parkhurst
Tel: 011 327 5883
Open: daily, noon–2am

Finding a decent place to play pool can be easier said than done, but you can call off the search party at Jolly Cool. With three tables to shoot some pool, place some bets and unleash that inner competitive streak fuelled by a few chilled beers, Jolly Cool is the perfect place to hang out with the guys. Order a drink at the bar while you wait your turn for a table, or sit outside and enjoy one of the bar's legendary pizzas. Just be sure to smother it in Jolly Cool's

signature peri-peri sauce. Decent tunes add to Jolly Cool's, er, cool factor.

### The Jolly Rodger *(right)*
10 4th Avenue, Parkhurst
Tel: 011 442 3954
Open: daily, 11am–1am

A bastion of England in the heart of South Africa, The Jolly Rodger champions traditional English pub life with smoky interiors and live sport showing on multiple screens. As you can imagine, the crowd is a rowdy bunch with first-year students and ex-pats drinking and cheering their way through booze-fuelled evenings. Split across two tiers – the top with a balcony overlooking the city – The Jolly Rodger is all about winding down, having fun and making as much noise as possible while doing it. A free jukebox in the corner adds to a riotous evening.

### Katzy's *(middle)*
The Firs, Corner of Oxford Road & Bierman Av, Rosebank
Tel: 011 880 3945
www.thegrill.co.za
Open: daily, 5.30pm (6.30pm Sat)–1am

New York comes to Jo'burg in the fabulous form of Katzy's, arguably South Africa's finest jazz club. Found in Rosebank's posh Firs mall, Katzy's is the perfect place to come for a pre- or post-dinner drink and a couple of well-cut cigars. Resident musicians entertain a classy crowd with live jazz, while a bar stocked with over 100 whisky brands ensures that drinkers stay long after the music has wrapped up. The interior is oh-so Greenwich Village with exposed brick walls adorned with jazz posters and more luscious leather sofas and dark wood tables than you can shake a saxophone at. Enjoy din-

ner at the equally New York The Grill-house (see Eat) first, found opposite.

### Melrose Arch Hotel (top)
### Pool Bar and Library Bar
1 Melrose Square, Melrose Arch
Tel: 011 214 6666
www.africanpridehotels.com/
melrose-arch-hotel
Open: daily, 9am–7pm

Set in the super-stylish Melrose Arch Hotel, the Pool Bar is so very South Beach Miami and a no-brainer when it comes to supping drinks in the glorious sunshine. Tables and chairs are even built into the shallow end of the pool, with patrons rolling up their trousers and enjoying their cocktails ankle-deep, while tunes are pumped out from underwater à la Delano. The hotel's 24-hour Library Bar, however, is best used in the winter, with a cosy ambience and a bar serving cigars and cognac to a classy, upwardly-mobile clientele. Once you've propped up the bar for long enough, consider dinner at the hotel's restaurant or hankering down in one of its many sumptuous suites.

### Metro Café & Bar (left)
Upper Level, Benmore
Shopping, 11th Avenue, Benmore
Tel: 011 883 2304
www.metrorestaurant.co.za
Open: daily, noon–2am

Dark, sexy and decadent, the bar, or self-styled 'Ultra Lounge', at Metro Café & Bar sets an entirely different mood to its downstairs restaurant.

Located at Benmore Shopping Centre, the interiors are all about dripping chandeliers, ornate wallpaper, comfortable sofas, deep red banquettes and contemporary wood paneling. Glass windows partition drinkers from the diners below reeling them in for postprandial digestifs. The seductive décor attracts a well-heel crowd who come and sink into the sofas, cocktail in hand and chat and flirt their way through to the early hours of the morning. Expect to jostle for space at the bar.

### The Polo Lounge (right)
### at The Westcliff Hotel
67 Jan Smuts Avenue, Westcliff
Tel: 011 481 6064
www.westcliff.co.za
Open: daily, 11am–late

Set inside the super-smart Westcliff Hotel, The Polo Lounge is where the political and financial powerhouses of nearby Westcliff congregate to talk business and bullshit. Cigars and cognac are optional, of course, but are positively encouraged to fit in with the aristocratic vibe. Unlike its namesake at the Beverly Hills Hotel, The Polo Lounge is decked out in a chic neo-colonial theme to remind its patrons that they are, in fact, in Africa and not in Los Angeles. Knock back champagne at the bar or step outside onto the legendary pool deck to soak up panoramic views over wealthy Westcliff, sundowner in-hand. Don't be intimidated by the sheer scale of the hotel; bar-goers will be driven up to the lounge once they've clocked-in at reception.

*drink...*

**The Radium Beerhall** *(top)*
282 Louis Botha Ave,
Orange Grove
Tel: 011 728 3866
www.theradium.co.za
Open: daily, 10am–1am

The Radium Beerhall is the oldest surviving bar in Jo'burg and it shows, with Western-style swing doors and prison-esque bars affixed to its windows. Wood abounds inside, from the teak bar through to the creaky floorboards underfoot, while nostalgic records and photos of the Radium's history adorn the walls. Attracting the young and old, the crowds here are split between propping up the bar and spilling onto the street outside – it doesn't seem to matter where one sits, so long as they can be part of the scene. Down whisky with some of the more established residents and ask a few questions about times gone by. Busy, sometimes raucous and a real spit and sawdust kind of place, Radium manages to keep the party going way past bedtime.

**The Troyeville Hotel** *(bottom)*
25 Bezuidenhout Street,
Troyeville
Tel: 011 402 7709
www.troyevillehotel.co.za
Open: daily, 9am–10pm

Set in the south of the CBD, this restaurant/bar concept is bit of a trek from Sandton but those who make the effort are rewarded with one of the best views of Jo'burg's skyline – particularly stunning at dusk. A favourite of artists, intellectuals and politicians, the bar offers a decent wine list and a selection of local beers, so chill and settle in for an alcohol-drenched afternoon. When the drinking gets a little too much the selection of Mozambican and Portuguese food goes a long way into filling the gaps and soaking up some of that excess booze. Recently nominated one of the top dining venues in South Africa, be rest assured anything you order is likely to be pretty damn fabulous.

# snack...

In addition to Jo'burg's excellent restaurants, there are a few small and stylish cafes perfect for grabbing a cup of coffee or a spot of lunch. We've summarized the best the city has to offer and chosen a range of places to satisfy your cravings at any time of the day. The following suggestions are all favorites with the locals, and we've covered everything from where to pick up a pizza at 2am to where to go when you want to splash out on an extravagant high tea.

Coffee culture has really hit the city in recent years and today there's no shortage of upmarket chains and unique delis popping up all over Jo'burg. Ladies-who-lunch are in their element and the suburbs of Parkhurst and Greenside have been flourished on the success of this new popular past-time. This in turn has spawned much more of a service culture where the managers/owners pride themselves on their loyal, local following and know they need to keep their customers on board.

For something simple, some of Jo'burg's top spots are found in the growing number of 'one size fits all' shopping centers. For a speedy caffeine fix, the Vida E franchise is the perfect choice, it's the Starbucks of South Africa and has outlets pretty much everywhere. The almost cultish Tashas restaurants are the perfect way to revive oneself after a shopping splurge or a fit of sightseeing; serving up

Love Cup Cake

snack…

modern takes on classic dishes (we love the Freezos). There are a few other chains that don't quite make the grade, but try Kauai for its healthy wraps and smoothies and the Col'Cachio chain for some of the city's best pizzas.

On the more traditional side is Fournos, a constantly-packed café where locals flock for the fresh breads and pastries and the continental-style deli counter. Similarly Dunkeld store is still family-run and has a great atmosphere.

While in Jo'burg step back to another era and try a classic afternoon tea. For the most decadent experience, take high tea at the Saxon Hotel or in The Conservatory at the Westcliff. The Saxon boasts spectacular gardens, while The Conservatory offers sumptuous three-tiered cake stands that will challenge even the most hardcore chocoholics.

A slightly lighter, but still stylish, tea or evening meal can be picked up at Annica's Deli or Stephanie's. Tucked away in the exclusive The Michelangelo Towers, Annica's menu ranges from cupcakes to caviar and draws in the city's wealthiest (and most attractive) ladies-who-lunch. Likewise Stephanie's offers some really delicious snacks for the sophisticats palate.

Finally, we had to mention the fabulous Andiccio's that opened in 2008. Inevitably at some point you'll end up wandering the streets in the early hours with a serious case of the munchies. Andiccio's is the perfect solution with its scrumptious pizzas, and don't worry, they won't judge your choice of toppings.

**Andiccio 24**  *(left)*
Greenside Quarters, Cnr of
Barry Hetzog and Gleneagles Road,
Greenside
Tel: 011 646 5359
www.andiccio24.co.za
Open: 24 hours daily

If you're wandering the streets of
Parkhurst or Greenside in the early
hours of the morning, Andiccio 24 is
the only place to head for a snack after a drink-or-ten. The long-suffering
staff show incredible resilience and,
for some unknown reason, happily put
up with their somewhat-inebriated clientele. Andiccio's doesn't restrict itself
to pizza and feeds up the drunk and the
stoned with pasta and Haagen-Dazs.
However, the totally customizable pizzas really are the star attraction. Just
keep adding the toppings as sobriety
and bizarre pregnancy-stye cravings
dictate – there have been some pretty special concoctions put together
at 3am. With a free delivery service
24 hours a day you don't even need
to leave the stoned comfort of your
sofa. A second branch can be found at
Sandton Court, Corner Rivonia Rd and
South Rd, Sandton tel: 011 783 8802.

**Annica's Deli**  *(top)*
The Michelangelo Towers,
Maude St, Sandton
Tel: 011 884 9445
www.annicas.co.za
Open: daily, 7am–10pm (4pm Sun)

Annica's Deli is a wonderfully decadent
patisserie located in the Michelangelo
Towers. Originally Annica's started life
as a bespoke cake-making enterprise,
but due to popular demand and a de-
voted clientele they opened up in this
smart development. The opulent interior décor and extravagant furnishings
belie the indulgence that waits inside.
The fantastic cakes on show all look
far too good to eat, they are more akin
to works of art ranging from beautiful,
towering, tiered creations adorned with
gold leaf to expertly crafted, delicate
lace-covered cupcakes. For those who
prefer something a bit heartier (or less
frou-frou) the chocolate rum brownies
are divine. Come sunset Annica's turns
into a charming restaurant offering a
classic South African/International
menu and a potently chic cocktail list.
And if you really feel like splashing
out there's a private lounge that serves
champagne and caviar.

**Bella**  *(right)*
66 Rivonia Road, Sandton
Tel: 011 883 6665
www.66rivonia.co.za
Open: 7.45am–3pm. Closed Sundays.

Located in the small 66 Rivonia Road
complex in the middle of Sandton,
Bella is a chic, Italian-style café-bis-
tro serving delicious breakfasts and
lunches to some of Jo'burg's smartest
customers. Owners Nikki and Vicki sell
a range of great gifts and a variety of
clever kitchen gadgets that are perfect
to take back home. Using only the
freshest, locally-sourced ingredients
the menu features mouth-watering organic salads and a variety of gourmet
open sandwiches; although they are really famous for their chicken and leek
pie, Norwegian salmon fishcakes and
tomato & feta tartlets. If you've still

snack...

got room left, the puddings will tempt even the strictest of dieters, the small-but-deadly hot chocolate cupcake and the baked cheesecake are just sinfully delicious.

___

### The Birdcage *(left)*
82 Jan Smuts Avenue, Saxonwold
Tel: 011 646 6315
Open: 9am–4pm. Closed Mondays.

Light lunches can sometimes be the most delicious, which is exactly what The Birdcage offers with its delicious deli-style café offering all kinds of little gastronomic treats. Only open for breakfast and lunch, diners help themselves to the selection of dishes from the counter, ranging from roast chicken right through to pies. For the super health conscious there is a salad bar, and for the sinfully indulgent an equally well-stocked and decadent dessert tray; highly recommended is the belt-busting chocolate brownie. The interior is eclectic to say the least with a collection of birdcages and crystal chandeliers hanging overhead. Sit inside close to the food, or outside in the tea garden under the shade of wilting trees.

___

### Chocodore *(middle)*
Cobbles Centre, Corner 4th Avenue and 11th Street, Parkhurst
Tel: 071 298 6102
Open: 9am–5pm Tues–Sat; 10am–4pm Sun–Mon

While chocolate might not be quite as good as sex, it does come a pretty close second. Chocodore, at Parkhurst's Cobbles Centre, is testament to this passion, with countless blends of the brown stuff on offer to those after something sticky and sweet. All hand-made and beautifully packaged, this is undoubtedly the best chocolate in the city; highly recommended is its signature croissant, filled to the brim with swirls of chocolate mousse. Wash it down with a combined strawberry and chocolate milkshake just to tip the scales in favour of that diabetic coma. Large-scale orders can be placed here for those hosting a party or celebrating something special. Just don't tell your guests you made them yourself – nobody will ever believe you.

**The Conservatory** *(right)*
The Westcliff Hotel,
67 Jan Smuts Avenue, Westcliff
Tel: 011 481 6000
www.westcliff.co.za
Open: daily, 9am–11pm

Part of the super-smart Westcliff Hotel, the Conservatory is a beautiful, light café with an al fresco pool terrace. In the autumn the views from the hotel terrace are wonderful with the Jacaranda trees are in bloom. The specialty of the Conservatory is the extremely rich and indulgent afternoon tea, (so make sure you have a light lunch and leave room) there's a classic or chocolate menu where the cakes, scones and éclairs are piled high on three-tiered stands. Lunch is equally as good and a tapas menu is served from 5pm. The

Conservatory is the perfect place for a quick bite to eat before splashing out on a bottle of champagne in the Polo Bar, with the rest of the city's movers and shakers. On a quiet afternoon if you are listening carefully you might be able to hear the roar of the lions in the Jo'burg Zoo a short distance away.

### ■ Contessa Tea    *(left)*
### ■ Shop
2a Rivonia Corner Shopping centre,
11th Avenue c/o Rivonia Boulevard
Tel: 011 234 6641
www.contessateashop.co.za
Open: 7.30am–4.30pm Mon-Fri;
8am–3pm Sat

Established in 2006, Contessa has really opened the world of specialty teas to South Africa. They have sourced loose tea and tea bags from around the globe – including varieties from China, the U.S.A, and Sri-Lanka. You'll be spoilt for choice with over 60 different choices on the carefully crafted menu – for those who want a take out, they retail the entire Twinings range as well as its own, beautifully packaged, Contessa selection. The traditional décor is simple, with a bold checkerboard floor and antique wooden chairs that give the café a laid-back feel. Contessa's the perfect spot to recharge your batteries. In addition to the fabulous teas — served in elegant glass teapots – they offer light lunches, a selection of homemade cakes and an extensive breakfast menu. The mince, egg and cheese on toast is surprisingly good!

snack...

### I Love Cup Cake *(right)*
Cobbles Centre, Corner 4th
Avenue and 11th Street, Parkhurst
Tel: 071 121 6234
www.ilovecupcake.co.za
Open: 9am (10am Mon)–5.30pm
Mon–Fri; 9am–3pm Sat; 10am–1pm
Sun

I Love Cup Cake channels its passion
into a range of delectable cupcakes,
all offered at its stand-alone store in
Parkhurst's Cobbles Centre. Decked
out in bright pink, the store itself is a
great place to debate about which of
the 18 different varieties to try first.
Those with a sweet tooth are bound to
be satisfied with something and if that
fails then just pop next door to, Chocodore (see page 98) for some chocolate. I Love Cupcake even operates a
takeaway service for those ordering
batches for parties and events or those
whose cup cake addiction now pre-
vents them from leaving home. Just try
not to salivate over them before your
guests have had a look in.

### Junipa *(middle)*
Shop G1, Hobart Centre, Cor-
ner or Grosvenor Street and Hobart
Street, Bryanston
Tel: 011 706 2387
Open: daily, 7am–4pm (2pm Sat, 1pm
Sun)

Started in a garage 12 years ago, Ju-
nipa has grown to become arguably
the best deli in Jo'burg – or at least
the most popular. Specialising in baked
goods, as well as a ridiculously extensive range of sandwiches, pastas and
salads, it's no wonder workers

congregate her during suspiciously long lunch hours. Sit indoors or outside under crisp umbrellas, bask in the sun on the veranda and enjoy one of Jo'burg's most understated success stories.

### Life *(top)*
Studio 104, Upper Level, Nelson Mandela Square, Sandton City, Sandton
Tel: 011 783 5965  www.life.za.org
Open: 8am (8.30 am Sat)–5pm.
Closed Sundays.

Life is the brainchild of an eponymous design firm specialising in hotels, restaurants and stores. This is immediately obvious at their own-brand café situated in their Mandela Square emporium which acts as a showroom for their interiors and furniture tucked away on the upper level. Outside of the edgy modern design, Wallpaper* style furniture and gleaming counter, Life offers weary shoppers the chance to sit down, relax and refuel with delicious deli-style offerings. The menu offers sandwiches, salads and sushi for a simple but delicious lunch, or simply sit back with a smoothie and watch the world go by from the comfort of a seat overlooking Nelson Mandela Square.

### Moemas Postma *(right)*
Corner of 3rd and 7th Avenues, Parktown North
Tel: 011 788 7725  www.moemas.co.za
Open: 7am–6pm Mon-Fri;
8am–4pm Sat; 9am–4pm Sun

Like many of Jo'burg's successful little spots, this family-run café-bakery is found in a small shopping centre. However, try not to be put off by the location, because once you get inside you'll be swept away by the café food and charming service. There are only 5 tables, so arrive early if you want to grab some lunch. Moemas Postma prides itself on using the finest, locally-sourced products and the food is always beautifully presented. The main attractions are undoubtedly the cakes, pastries and baked treats artfully displayed in the windows to entice passing shoppers. Thanks to pastry chef Danielle's eight years of training, the Nutella tartlets and carrot cake are now renowned throughout Jo'burg. If you're feeling health conscious, then the salad bar is the perfect antidote to the calorie-laden patisseries.

### Red Mango *(left)*
Shop 27, The Piazza, Melrose Arch, Melrose
Tel: 011 684 1058
www.redmangosa.com
Open: daily, 8am–5pm

Red Mango is a growing chain that is quickly gaining popularity amongst South Africa's health-conscious crowd. They serve up a rather smug range of all things healthy, although the main draw is their delicious, natural, fat-free, cholesterol-free frozen yogurt served with fresh fruit toppings. If you're after something on the run then the wonderfully fresh juices and slightly more indulgent smoothies are perfect. Alternatively, for those feeling particularly puckish, try the wholesome sandwiches. The interior at the Melrose Arch

snack...

branch is a little more stylish than the others and there's a great view over the piazza below from the balcony.

### The Saxon *(top)*
36 Saxon Road, Sandhurst
Tel: 011 292 6000
www.thesaxon.com
Open: daily, 3pm–5pm

One of the city's top hotels, the Saxon is a great place to spend an afternoon indulging in an extravagant high tea. The hotel has claimed the title of 'World's Leading Boutique Hotel' for the last six consecutive years (although we're not entirely sure who hands out these titles), and it really is worth a visit even if you don't choose to stay here yourself. The afternoon tea menu is the cheapest way to get a taste of the Saxon's style and is definitely best enjoyed on the wonderfully peaceful pool terrace. Then, as the sun sets switch over to the cocktail menu and watch the wonderfully changing hues as the huge African sun dips below the horizon. The attentive staff will make sure that you're well looked after.

### Stephanie's *(middle)*
Lower Level, 24 Hyde Park Shopping Centre, Hyde Park
Tel: 011 325 4039
Open: 9am–6pm Mon-Sat;
10am–1pm Sun

Located in the Hyde Park Shopping Centre, this stylish restaurant is a Jo'burg institution. Nestled among some of the city's most exclusive shops, it's easily recognizable by the chic black and white design and large patio-style umbrellas. Inside, the elegant, European atmosphere makes it a popular choice among the ladies-who-lunch. We think that Stephanie's is best visited for a lazy breakfast; many people think that they serve up the best eggs benedict in town. For those more concerned about their waistline the health breakfast hits the mark, but really the cappuccinos, cakes and scones are not to be missed. It's the perfect spot to refuel before or after hitting the shops, and the queues on a Saturday morning are certainly a testament to the level of service and quality.

### Tashas *(bottom)*
Atholl Square, Corner of Katherine St and Wierda Road East, Sandton
Tel: 011 884 0365
www.tashascafe.com
Open: 6.30am–6pm Mon-Sat;
7.30am–4pm Sun

Ever since the opening of the first Tashas café in Atholl Square, the company has gone from strength to strength. With a mission to provide quality ingredients, friendly service, and innovative, affordable food, Tashas has become a firm favourite with sceney locals and the original branch still remains extremely popular. Simply but beautifully decorated, the restaurants offer a relaxed European-style atmosphere. The chain has also introduced the unusual idea of hanging decorative tableware from the ceiling, depending on the branch knives and forks, paper cups or even napkins could be dangling over your table. However,

snack...

what really draws in the crowds is the mouth-watering menu, offering everything from refreshing fruit granitas to sophisticated grilled salmon. Not to mention the comfort-eating classics such as fish cakes, hot dogs and fish & chips. If you're after something a bit different, try the *quesadillas* or the 'breakfast in bed' – accompanied, of course, by the perfect cappuccino. Just beware Tashas are very popular, and you might have to queue for your lunch. Additional branches can be found at the Melrose Arch Centre, Village View Shopping Centre and at 23 Morningside Shopping Centre.

---

**Vida E** *(top)*
24 Central, Corner Fredman & Gwen Lane, Sandton
Tel: 011 884 5996
www.vidaecaffe.com
Open: daily, 7am–5pm

This great franchise now has branches across South Africa. It's pretty much Jo'burg's equivalent of Starbucks, since you order and pay your coffee at the bar. However, the friendly, helpful staff and the buzzing atmosphere really sets Vida E apart from its competitors – especially when you tip, when the servers all perform a cheer in unison. The Sandton Central venue in particular is a great place to grab a coffee, either relaxing outside on wooden decking under shady trees or collapsing at a table inside. Either way, it's a great urban retreat and a welcome alternative to the many shopping centre based cafés in the city. Additional branches can also be found in Greenside, Parktown and OR Tambo Airport.

**Wild Olive** *(bottom)*
14 Gleneagles Road, Greenside
Tel: 011 646 1445
Open: 8.30am–5.30pm (3.30pm Sat/Sun). Closed Mondays.

This quaint little deli is set on the main street in Greenside and has long been a favourite among the city's foodies. There's a wide range home-cooked goodies on sale to be taken home, from rusks and muesli to delicious biscuits, nougats and chocolates. If you want to eat here, then you can choose from seats outside on the pavement, inside, or in the cute courtyard garden out back. The menu offers simple, and beautifully prepared, home-cooked food. For breakfast the muesli (with either honey, healthy or nuts) costs just R6 per bowl and is particularly wholesome. The cooked breakfast is definitely worth a try, especially the omelettes. For lunch there's an extensive buffet on offer, comprising a range of salads, quiches and delicious sandwiches.

snack...

# party...

There's no denying that Jo'burg knows how to party, with clubs that range from super-stylish to downright dirty. In an effort to fuel the local economy, locals waste no time in hitting up the clubs on Thursday, Friday and Saturday nights – even though things do seem to wrap up fairly early, normally at around midnight. Jo'burg doesn't have the big clubs synonymous with the Northern hemisphere – in fact, you can more or less count the superclubs on one hand – but when you do find them they are generally extremely well-run, with tough security on the doors to keep the riff-raff out and the ra-ras in. With affordable drinks and a friendly party crowd enjoying themselves on the dance floor you're almost guaranteed the night's going to get a little bit raucous. There are, of course, exceptions with certain venues in a city notorious for its drugs 'n' thugs culture, but these have been excluded from our selection as nobody wants to go home at the end of the night an unflattering shade of black-and-blue.

When it comes to clubbing, age is but a number and there's a wide spectrum of generations out and about at any given club at any given time. That said, as a general rule of thumb the larger the club the younger the crowd; smaller clubs tend to attract more mature crowds, while the bigger ones are full of energetic, bright young things. Music-wise, Jo'burg couldn't be more varied; from jazz to rock, dance to pop, the city has it all. Unlike some places, the clubs' music policy is, well, eclectic – basically, their DJs play whatever the hell they want. With many of the city's main clubs found outside of Sandton Central, revellers need to get a taxi there and back. This can be pre-arranged by most hotels, so fear not – you won't need to walk. If you want to arrive in superstar style, however – and let's face it, who doesn't? – then a number of Limo companies and luxury transfer services are at-hand to whisk you about like a celebrity. If you're heading to a club in the CBD, be sure to pre-arrange your return home by getting the driver's mobile number on your way there – you don't want to be lost downtown late at night.

icci Beach

party…

But pulling up in style isn't enough. Many of Jo'burg's clubs come with a strict dress code and lashings of attitude at the door, clubbers are advised to pull out all the stops and dress to impress. Another local rule suggests the further out of Sandton a club is the slacker the dress code and the cheaper the drinks. In general, though, guys should wear leather shoes and collared shirts to avoid disappointment. Meanwhile, skyscraper heels and barely-legal skirts will have ladies ducking beneath the velvet ropes withl ease. Cash can be used as normal once inside, but more often than not you can run tabs at the bar with a card.

So where to go for what? If you're looking to knock 'em back, then get up on the tables head to Rose Boys. If you're after credible music, then head to Tokyo Star. If you want mainstream, it's Movida all the way. And if you want to rub shoulders with Jo'burg's top movers and shakers, then check out A-list hangouts Taboo and Moloko. Feeling exotic? You can do worse than grinding to the Latin beats at Latinova. Reckon you have a chance with the fash pack? Then there's nowhere more fabulous than Fashion TV Café. In the mood for live music? Then listen to jazz at The Bassline or the Blues Room. Those with dancing feet should bust some moves at Truth, or get wet 'n' wild at sweatier spots E.S.P. and Nicci Beach. Looking for adult entertainment? Then slink into Teazers or The Grand for some XXX-rated excitement.

One word of warning; although Jo'burgers are generally friendly, be reminded that this is still an extremely dangerous city. Tensions generally arise from the city's macho 'gym culture', and as a result of different cultures living together in close proximity. The guys have attitude and don't take kindly to being bounced around, or to their ladies being picked up – especially by foreigners. Be street-wise and don't rely on your accent to wrangle your way out of a sticky situation; the city already has a melting pot of accents, and a clipped English voice won't charm anyone. That said, ladies can expect to be spoilt by locals.

**The Bassline** *(top-left)*
10 Henry Nxumalo Street, Newton
Tel: 011 838 9145 www.bassline.co.za
Open: 8pm–2am Weds–Sat

One of Jo'burg's better-known clubs, The Bassline is located in the CBD and has a simple strapline that sums it up nicely – 'In Music We Trust'. With a strong affinity to jazz, the venue prides itself on showcasing some of South Africa's best talent, and is packed out with music-loving spectators every Friday and Saturday night. Complete with friendly bar staff and an equally friendly clientele, this is just the ticket for those with a passion for live music. Because of its location, pre-arrange a car back to your hotel before you go.

.................................................................

**E.S.P** *(bottom-left)*
84 Oxford Road, Corner of Eton Street and Ferndale, Randburg
Tel: 011 792 4110 www.esp.co.za
Open: 10pm 'til late Saturdays.

As one of the longest-running dance clubs in South Africa – 14 years, to be precise – it's no surprise that E.S.P. has a legion of loyal supporters. Cramming hours of dance, trance and house music into just one Saturday evening per week, club-goers can expect a side order of sweat with their Sambuca at this multi-floored establishment. With such a good reputation for credible club

music, it's no wonder the likes of Tiesto, Sebastian Ingrosso, Sonique and Benny Benassi have played here. Take your shirt off and wave your hands in the air like you just don't care if you want to fit in.

......................................................................

Gin *(middle)*
12 Gleneagles Road, Greenside
Tel: 084 555 9585
www.gingin.co.za
Open: 8am–2am Mon–Sat

Gin is often described as a mother's ruin, but it doesn't seem to ruin much at its eponymous club, a trendy Jo'burg nightspot with an emphasis on gin-based cocktails. Located in Greenside,

Gin is a hot hangout for those who like good drinks and good music served up in equal measures. Bop downstairs to the beats of the live DJ, or relax upstairs on the balcony during the sticky summer months – gin and ice-cold tonic in-hand, of course.

......................................................................

Fashion TV Café *(right)*
Shop P1, Michaelangelo Towers Mall, Maude Street, Sandton
Tel: 011 783 1866
www.ftvsandton.co.za
Open: 5pm 'til late Weds–Sat

Part of Fashion TV's international chain of chic cafés, FTV Café in Sandton is as sought after as you might expect with style mavens flocking in their droves to see and be seen. Attracting a cookie-cutter crowd of mostly male and female models, the food is kept light and healthy with plenty of sushi on offer and an extensive cocktail list for those who prefer a liquid-only diet (and lets' face it, what model doesn't?). Local DJs take to the decks after dinner, when the equally high-heeled clientele purr around the floor in their designer finery. Thursdays are particularly busy, so book a table to ensure you get a space for the evening. With a door policy that won't admit anyone under 23, this is fabulous yuppie fun at its most exclusive.

 **Latinova** *(left)*
160 Jan Smuts, Corner of 7th Ave and Jan Smuts
Tel: 011 447 1006
www.latinovasa.com
Open: 10pm 'til late. Fri/Sat

If you like the idea of hot, heady nights set against pulsing Latino music, then Latinova should be the hangout for you. Located above the ultra-exclusive Louis XI restaurant, Latinova carries on the theme of over-the-top opulent décor with red velvet curtains and dazzling filigree wallpaper. Dancing is the club's raison d'etre, with a raised platform that stages flamenco, salsa and latino dancing, as well as performances from live bands. As you can imagine, Latinova attracts a sexy crowd of young revellers in barely-there outfits who come to grind with sultry strangers. Join them and quench your thirst for a little taste of Havana right here in Jo'burg.

 **The Manhattan Club** *(right)*
19 Wessels Road, Rivonia
Tel: 011 803 7085
www.manhattanclub.co.za
Open: daily, 8pm–2am.

The Manhattan Club keeps young Jo'burgers partying hard on an enormous dance floor amid swish surroundings. As the largest club in Sandton it's heaving pretty much every night of the week, with a high-tech light and sound system to accompany the commercial tracks spun by the ever-changing roster of DJs. There are eight bars in total, including a dedicated shooters bar, a smoking bar selling whisky and cigars, and a cocktail bar reserved exclusively for ladies. Party hard and party fast, or risk looking like an old codger.

**Moloko** *(bottom)*
160 Jan Smuts Avenue, Corner 7th Avenue, Rosebank
Tel: 011 447 1082
www.molokojoburg.com
Open: 9pm–late Thurs–Sat.

If it's hip it's happening, and Moloko is certainly hip so make sure you're happening – sharp suits for gents, barely-there dresses for ladies – to ensure entry. Located in Rosebank's self-proclaimed 'Design District', the interiors are suitably stylish with contemporary décor that extends through to its long bar and lounge area. Think ornate wallpapers, Persian rugs and fabulously flattering lighting. The dance floor, meanwhile, is manned by DJs who know what they're doing, with house, R&B and Kwaitio (a genre of house music combined with distinctly African

party...

beats) dominating the sound system. Whisky, cognac and Champagne are the order of the day here, so prop up the bar and drink with the best of 'em.

### ■ Movida *(left)*
Rivonia Crossing, Corner of Rivonia Rd and Witkoppen, Sunninghill
Tel: 011 234 8000
www.movida.co.za
Open: 9pm 'til late Fri/Sat

Moulin Rouge is the inspiration behind Movida, a super-stylish theatre-cum-club-cum-cocktail bar. The multi-purpose venue makes for quite the night out, with the music stopping abruptly on any given evening to make way for an impromptu cabaret performance – before cranking up the club music again and turning back into a club. The music itself is commercial, but the DJs here know how to work both the decks and the crowds to get the whole place rocking. The interiors are wonderfully decadent (if just a little bit kitsch), with deep reds and moody lighting making for a sultry space indeed. And with an age restriction enforced at the door – ladies need to be at least 23, while gents can be no younger than 25 – this is a truly grown-up night out.

**Nicci Beach** *(middle)*
Wild Waters Complex,
1 Margaret Street, Bardene, Boksburg
Tel: 011 823 5714
www.niccibeach.co.za
Open: noon–2am Fri/Sat; noon–midnight Sun

Not to be confused with upscale beach club Nikki Beach, Nicci Beach is more about fun than class – but it's still worth checking out. In fact, it's home to some of Jo'burg's hottest al fresco dance parties and is one of the only instances where you can get wild without getting wet in the middle of a water park. It's all very Vegas, set against swaying palms and overlooking the wave pool, but live music saves its credibility somewhat. Head to Nicci Beach on a Sunday for sundowners and a languid supper on the wooden decking.

**Rose Boys** *(right)*
Corner of Oxford Road and
Corlett Drive, Illovo
Tel: 011 880 9989
Open: 5pm–2am Mon–Sat

There's something a little bit rebellious about Rose Boys, a bar described by its owner Kerry Edgar as a "nice little hole in the wall." The décor is suitably eclectic, with a black-and-pink checkerboard entrance and interiors decked

*party...*

out with statues, chandeliers and paintings. Managed by Kerry herself, you can guarantee the bar is run exactly as she planned; superb cocktails served up against a backdrop of tunes that range from jazz to Bob Sinclar. The one thing that does offend her otherwise happy patrons, however, are the drink prices, which vary from order to order. If you're lucky enough to order from the landlady herself, she does reward loyalty by lowering the prices on every round you buy. There's no logic or purpose to this, it's just what Kerry wants. And what Kerry wants, Kerry gets – including a hugely popular haunt crammed with a crowd that lap up the chaos.

**Taboo** *(right)*
24 Central, Corner of Fredman Drive and Gwen Lane, Sandton
Tel: 011 783 2200
www.taboo.co.za
Open: 7pm 'til late. Fri/Sat

If you must get into trouble, do it at Taboo. Spread across a number of decadently designed floors, Taboo is all about being seen against a backdrop of stylish décor and a state-of-the-art sound and light system. Its best feature, however, is a rooftop with sweeping views out over Sandton Central and a bar set beneath a beautiful Bedouin tent. With free-flowing champagne and cocktails on offer, the dance floor and VIP areas are never short of South Africa's most beautiful locals. As the king of reinvention, Taboo tries to

mix things up at the weekend with a host of different parties and events. Be sure to dress well – the bouncers take no prisoners.

**Tokyo Star** *(top)*
Shop 1 Comtec House, 26 Gleneagles Road, Greenside
Tel: 084 208 0236
www.tokyostar.co.za
Open: 9pm 'til late Fri/Sat

Anime and plenty of plastic are the order of the day at Tokyo Star, an Asian-inspired destination bar in Greenside. Once a Mecca for casual partygoers in Old Melville, its new location doesn't mean it's lost any of its cool credentials – it has simply grown up, with classier interiors and an equally chic clientele that has replaced the Converses with smart shoes and heels. Talented DJs pump out a mix of old and new hits that span genres, while a bar serves up drinks such as Jaegermeister are more than reasonable. Just watch out for the 10 per cent surcharge when paying with a credit card – cheeky buggers!

**Truth** *(bottom)*
OId Snake Park,
Old Pretoria Road, Midrand
Tel: 011 315 9295
www.truthjhb.com
Open: 10pm 'til late Friday and Saturday. Check the site for gigs first.

Regarded as South Africa's number-one underground superclub, Truth has been on the scene for quite some

119

time and has showcased some of the world's most prestigious superstar DJs. Pumping out pure dance and electronic music to an eager crowd of revellers, this is arguably the best venue in Jo'burg for busting some moves on any one of the number of dance floors. There's even an outside dance floor in the quad, should you want to strip off a layer or two and shimmy under the stars. Housed in an old snake park, the club is made up of winding corridors and a maze of rooms once used for exhibits – be sure not to get lost after you've had a few! Truth is a 30-minute drive from Sandton Central, but easy to find. Just look out for the cars and lights.

## Live Music

### Blues Room
Village Walk Shopping Centre, Corner of Maude Street and Rivonia Road, Sandton
Tel: 011 784 5527
www.bluesroom.co.za
Open: 7pm 'til midnight Weds–Sat

The Blues Room is a long-standing venue that has supported jazz and blues for over 15 years. The club is set in a basement in the centre of Village Walk Shopping Centre in Sandton Central, but that's not to say it's any less upmarket. Serving up decent food alongside plenty of live entertainment – including jazz, blues, rock 'n' roll and comedy – it attracts an older, mostly white crowd.

# Adult Entertainment

### Teazers *(right)*
344 Rivonia Boulevard, Rivonia
Tel: 011 807 8722
www.teazers.co.za
Open: 6pm–'til late Mon–Thurs; 12.30pm–'til late Fri; 6pm–late Sat.

Arguably the most famous strip club chain in South Africa, the founder of Teazers proves that sex sells with a large empire behind him and women dangling off him – like a South African Peter Stringfellow, if you will. His clubs keep gents happy with a roster of lovely ladies, whether dancing on tables or entertaining in private booths. Somewhat surprisingly for a strip club, Teazers serves lunch as well as dinner to cater for actual appetites as well as sexual ones. Ladies aren't left out, either; Teaze-hers is around the corner, and caters to female eyes with a host of oiled-up chaps.

### The Grand
Corner of Main Rivonia Road and 11th Avenue, Rivonia, Sandton
Tel: 011 234 9593
Open: 6pm 'til late Mon–Thurs; 12.30pm–late Fri

Strip clubs and style don't usually stroll hand-in-hand, but The Grand breaks the mould with a chic club that claims to be one of the largest joints of its kind in the world. Conveniently located in Rivonia, the club is a spacious affair with a number of stages and bars as well as a large dining area for patrons to enjoy. Entry is R300 depending on what time you arrive, but this includes

dinner. Highly recommended are the caviar, sushi and curry – not necessarily together. Dances range from R500 to R2,500.

ensures your night goes on and on – quite literally, in this instance, with an evening effect replicated inside.

party…

### Montecasino
Montecasino Boulevard,
Fourways, Sandton
Tel: 011 510 7000
www.montecasino.co.za
Open: 24 hours daily

Montecasino is located in Fourways, and is unquestionably Jo'burg's top entertainment destination, having being voted Best Casino, Best Entertainment Complex, Best Cinema Complex and Best place to take out-of-towners in a series of impressive accolades. The setting is about as far from Africa as you can get, with its interiors looking a little like a Medieval town in Italy. Whether you're gambling on the slot machines, eating or drinking, this place

# culture...

Jo'burg has no culture ... Well, that's the belief of many South Africans. We disagree, culture doesn't have to be all about museums and galleries, culture is about life, history and experience and we, here in Jo'burg, know all about that. For the more grown up and sensitive hedonist (i.e. life is no longer about the next high be it alcohol, food or sex) then there are variety of treats. The theatrical tradition is strong in the city with visiting international companies setting the bar high and local ones responding with equal calibre.

Art has been typically seen as the preserve of the elite (you have to remember the *braai* is the right of passage out here) and like any good art scene the openings of important exhibitions are patronised by those who should be/need to be seen as well as the dilettanti both professional and amateur. There are numerous art galleries and museums to visit, places such as the Everard Read and Goodman in Rosebank have been around for many years and exhibit some of the best and most expensive art. To find out the gallery listings buy the Mail or Guardian newspaper to get an up-to-date glimpse. For the more adventurous visit the townships to see the true local artists (it's not the same as it used to be, we promise), favouring distinctive African styles and mediums.

For something off the beaten cultural track, the Jo'burg Zoo is a fantastic day out, or even better, take a more personal night time tour to see the more elusive creatures and learn first hand from the zoo keepers what makes them tick. Not far from the Zoo is the War Museum where visitors can see both ancient and modern artefacts that shaped the world, after all, until very recently, South Africa has been a battle ground spanning centuries of civilization starting with early man and going up to the state-sponsored bush wars in neighbouring countries, only really ending in the last decade.

If you can take the time to travel outside of Jo'burg try and get to the 'Cradle of Human Kind'. Here you can check into the Maropeng tourism centre and learn about the origin of man. For those interested in the political history of our country, then you should visit the Apartheid Museum and the Hector Pieterson Memorial – both offering a chilling reminder of an oppressive regime. Take a tour into one of the townships and see how millions of South Africans live away from their gated communities, private security companies and air-conditioned taxis.

INKUNDLA YOMGAQOSISEKO
INKANTOLO YOMTHETHOSISEKELO
KHOTO YA VUMBIWA
INKANTOLO YEMITSETFOSISEKELO
KGOROTSHEKO YA MOLAOTHEO
IXHOTHO YOMTHETHOSISEKELO
CONSTITUTIONAL COURT
GOTLA LA DINYEWE LA MOLAOTHEO
KHOTHE YA NDAYOTEWA
KONSTITUSIONELE HOF
KGOTLATSHEKELO YA MOLAOTHEO

culture...

# Sightseeing

**Apartheid Museum** *(left)*
Northern Parkway and Gold
Reef Road, Johannesburg
Tel: 011 309 4700
www.apartheidmuseum.org
Open: 10am–5pm Tues–Sun

A thirty-minute drive from Sandton, situated between the Jo'burg CBD and Soweto, this is an incredibly powerful and emotional museum. Housed within the interesting architecture are a collection documents that testify to the atrocities committed against black South Africans during the segregation imposed by the Nationalist Government regime between 1948 and 1994. The museum is full of chilling reminders of this period, including passbooks, cages and the symbolic 121 hangmen's nooses. The museum attempts to give visitors an insight into every day township life during the 1970s through the use of photography and original video footage.

**Constitution Hill** *(middle)*
Constitutional Court, Between
Joubert Stand Kotze, Braamfontein,
Jo'burg

Tel: 011 381 3100
www.constitutionhill.org.za
Open: 9am–5pm Mon-Fri;
10am–3pm Sat

Built on the site of the Old Fort Prison Complex, where Nelson Mandela, Mahatma Gandhi and numerous others were unjustly imprisoned and mistreated, Constitution Hill is now home to the democratic Constitutional Court of South Africa. The architecture is spectacular, a juxtaposition of original structures and contemporary additions. Guided tours are available too, tracing the history of the site back to the Boer War.

**Everard Read Gallery**  *(right)*

6 Jellicoe Avenue, Rosebank
Tel: 011 788 4805
www.everard-read.co.za
Open: 9am–6pm Mon–Fri;
9am–1pm Sat

This is considered by some to be the top gallery in Jo'burg and certainly the spot to come to if you are looking to understand and potentially purchase the cream of contemporary South African art. With a rich history dating back to the 1912, when Jo'burg was first becoming established as a mining town, it has since settled into the

125

architecturally aesthetic premises in Rosebank. For the past 30 years the gallery has been supporting local artists and sculptors from all walks of life. The exhibitions change on a regular basis and a recently built new wing has substantially extended the building allowing a greater range of objects to be displayed. Check the website for listings.

 **The Goodman Gallery** *(left)*
163 Jan Smuts Avenue, Parkwood
Tel: 011 788 1113
www.goodman-gallery.co.za
Open: 9.30am–5.30pm Tues–Fri; 9.30am–4pm Sat

One of the city's top contemporary art galleries, the Goodman is known for featuring many of the South African greats, the likes of Walter Battiss and Norman Catherine are often on display alongside a selection of more modern local artists. Stretching past the 30 year mark has been an accomplishment for the gallery and it is now recognized domestically and internationally as being a significant player in the art world. The exhibitions tend to be a little different to that those at the Everard Reed, however, since they are nearby eachother it makes for a cultured morning to explore both side by side and really gain an insight into African and South African art. Check the website for comprehensive listings.

**Hector Pieterson** *(right)*
**Memorial and Museum**
8287 Khumalo Street, Orlando West, Soweto

Tel: 011 536 2253
Open: daily, 10am–5pm (4pm Sun)

This particular museum marks the day of the Soweto uprising in 6 June 1976, within 100 meters of where the 12 year-old Hector was shot. He was made famous by the photographer, Sam Nzima, who, during the riots, captured an image of the young boy being carried, dying, in the arms of a fellow student along side his sister. The protest was in response to the imposition of Afrikaans on the curriculum throughout schools in the townships. Like the Apartheid Museum it does well bringing the era and the senseless human tragedy to life. Haunting images, videos and sounds of the period help visitors appreciate the daily struggles of the subjugated black population Guided tours are available.

 **Jo'burg Zoo** *(bottom)*
Jan Smuts Avenue, Parkview
Tel: 011 646-2000
www.jhbzoo.org.za
Open: daily, 8.30am–5.30pm

The Jo'burg Zoo, opened in 1904, is based around four basic principles – education, conservation, recreation and research. Beautifully designed and well maintained, the exhibits and enclosures work to bring visitors closer to many of the animals that cover our world. The animals are definitely not restricted to those found on the African continent and contain: big cats, bears, monkeys, snakes and all manner of smaller creatures. For a real treat, book an evening tour of the zoo. Guests are driven around by one of the vets in a tractor with carriages behind it, with

culture...

the idea being visitors will see a different side of the animals, as well as some of the more shy ones, all accompanied by expert commentary.

---

### Lesedi Village *(top)*
Portion 198 493 Kalkheuwel,
R512, Lanseria
Tel: 012 205 1394
www.lesedi.com
Open: Tours commence daily at
11.30am and 4.30pm

The Lesedi Cultural Village was established to provide an authentic showcase of the traditional cultures of some of the well-known African tribes, who have their home in South Africa. Representatives of these tribes were involved in the design of the villages to ensure an accurate, historically representative portrayal of their indigenous cultures. They are meant to showcase and highlight a more traditional way of life, day-to-day activities and give an intimate view of tribal rituals. The villages are lived in today by members of these communities, which serves to breathe life into their fascinating cultures. Situated within the Cradle of Humankind, Lesedi provides the visitor with a better understanding of the rich cultural background of the traditional peoples of South Africa.

---

### Maropeng *(middle)*
Maropeng Visitor Centre, on the R400, just off the R563 Hekpoort road, Cradle of Humankind, Magaliesberg
Tel: 014 577 9000
www.maropeng.co.za
Open: daily, 9am–5pm

The Maropeng visitor centre has won numerous awards for its informative, accessible and interactive exhibits. Situated in the Cradle of Mankind, the museum's aim is to inform visitors about the development of the humankind over the past few million years. It only takes an hour to get here from Sandton, and it really is worth a visit. A joint admission can also be purchased for the Sterkfontein Caves. These incredible caverns provided archaeologists with some groundbreaking discoveries, including 2 million year old tools and the famous fossils of 'Mrs Ples' and 'Little Foot'. Recently, the centre has also added an underground boat ride. This sensory journey will guide you back through the development of the Earth from the last ice age right back to the 'Big Bang'.

---

### Museum of *(bottom)*
### Military History
Erlswold Way, Saxonwold
Tel: 011 646 5513
www.militarymuseum.co.za
Open: daily, 9am–4.30pm

This magnificent museum, sitting next door to the Jo'burg Zoo, is a testament to South Africa's position as the predominant military power on the continent. The entrance to the museum is flanked by an impressive array of military vehicles from recent history. The exhibition inside comprises some 40,000 different items, demonstrating the country's bellicose past and acknowledgement of military might. However, these weapons have helped shape not only South Africa's immediate present but that of its neighbours and the world at large. The objects on

culture...

display range from some of the rarest aircraft on the planet to books, journals and archive material. The Museum is also regarded as the spiritual and a symbolic home for regular and reserve soldiers and veterans in South Africa and throughout the world. A number of veteran organisations view the Museum as their headquarters.

# Theatres

**Barnyard Theatre** *(bottom)*
Shop 40, Broadacres Shopping Centre, Cnr Cedar Avenue and Valley Road, Broadacres, Fourways
Tel: 011 467 6983
www.barnyardtheatre.co.za

Barnyard is a multi-faceted venue that hosts everything from musicians and local bands to comedians and theatrical performances. The idea is that you eat while you're being entertained – book a table, order a takeaway (yes, we're serious) or bring a picnic and get stuck into some serious drinking. The cover bands will get you up and dancing and the comedians will have you rolling in the aisles. I guess the concept is in the name – high culture it ain't, but hey it's fun.

**Jo'burg Civic Theatre**
158 Loveday Street, Braamfontein, Jo'burg
Tel: 011 877 6800
www.showbusiness.co.za

The Civic theatre has hosted many local and international companies putting on a variety of performances. These have included Broadway musi-cals, ballets and comedies, as well as a number of local shows highlighting South Africa's rich theatrical history, some of which have gone to become international successes. Situated in Braamfontein on the outskirts of the CBD. There is ample secure parking and security to ensure your safety in the area. There are regular changes to the program, so for up to date information on the pending shows, please refer to their website

**Market Theatre** *(top)*
56 Wolhuter St, Newtown
Tel: 011 832 1641
www.markettheatre.co.za

Founded in Jo'burg in 1976 and constructed from the remnants of Jo'burg's Indian Fruit Market, built in 1913, the space was active in the struggle against apartheid, becoming internationally renowned as South Africa's 'Theatre of the Struggle'. Today its programme presents past and present productions ranging from contemporary political dramas to classis anti-apartheid plays that have included Woza Albert, Asinamali, Bopha, Sophiatown, You Strike the Woman You Strike a Rock, Born in the RSA, Black Dog - Inj'emnyama, as well as the premieres of many of Athol Fugard's award-winning dramas.

*culture...*

### The Old Mutual Theatre on The Square

Nelson Mandela Square, Sandton
Tel: 011 883 8606
www.theatreonthesquare.co.za

The Old Mutual Theatre on The Square is a 200-seat often described as the life and soul of Nelson Mandela Square. The programme contains a range of domestic and international plays that appeal to the slightly more high-brow residents of Sandton. Pre or post-performance there are a range of restaurants in walking distance, the best being Wang Thai or The Butcher's Grill (see Eat).

Park and is similar to the Star chain showing blockbuster and mainstream films.

### Ster Kinekor

Ground Floor, Sandton City, Rivonia Road, Sandton
Tel: 0861 300 444
www.ster-kinekor.co.za

The Ster Kinekor movies house in Sandton City has 11 screens showing the latest blockbuster movies an d has the technology to show 3D films. There is another branch in The Zone Shopping Centre in Rosebank.

## Cinemas

### Cinema Nouveau

Level 1, Rosebank Mall, Cnr. Bath & Baker Streets, Rosebank
Tel: 0861 300 444
www.sterkinekor.com

An art cinema franchise of the Star Kinekor chain that shows many world cinema films, as well as a selection of more specialised local films. The Nouveau has been known to host a few film festivals as well as retrospective or themed seasons.

### Nu Metro

Hyde Park Shopping Centre, Jan Smuts Avenue, Hyde Park
Tel: 011 325 4257
www.numetro.co.za

This is the only cinema in the Hyde

# notes…

# shop...

Despite being home to some of the world's showiest houses and flashiest cars, many Jozis use the spending power of their credit cards to finance their hedonistic lifestyles – with locals referring to this slice of stylish paradise as the 'credit ghetto.' That said, visitors will find that shopping in Jo'burg can be done at a fraction of the cost you're used to – even if some of the more upmarket international brands can be slightly more expensive than back home.

With their love of spending, it's no surprise that Jozis like looking good in the latest threads, which is why the city is brimming with boutiques for label-loving ladies and gents. Fuelling their insatiable appetite for material goods is an ever-increasing number of shopping centres, with new malls seemingly popping up by the day. For your convenience, all the shops featured here have been chosen for their proximity to our recommended hotels – if not within walking distance, you'll find all of them just a short taxi ride away. Limousines, of course, can be hired for true diva-like behaviour.

The major shopping areas are Rosebank, Hyde Park, Sandton, Melrose and Morningside, with other noteworthy outlets in Parkhurst and on 44 Stanley Street. It may also be worth checking out Fourways Mall and Eastgate Mall, just in case you can't get something at any of the other places on our retail hit-list. Please also note that most shopping centres have an on-site tax office to ensure you get money back on your purchases before you jet out of the country. And let's face it, we all like a little rebate.

Finally, as any true hedonist knows, sometimes pounding the pavement is just too much hard work – particularly when wearing designer soles. Which is why personal shopping is also included below, to ease the stresses of strains of spending your own money yourself. You can even have your wares brought over to your hotel should you not want to leave the comfort of your fine thread-count sheets. After all, that's what an Hg2 city break's all about isn't it?

shop...

# Sandton

### Legacy Corner Mall
Nelson Mandela Square, Sandton

Located on 5th Avenue and Maude Street, Legacy Corner Mall was built to complement the existing retails facilities of adjacent Nelson Mandela Square. High-end retail outlets, dining facilities, a hotel and apartments finish things off nicely.

**The Vault**  The impactful shop fitting elements and interior of this high end trend shop reiterates the level of clothing found within in it. Located in the exclusive, new, Legacy Corner shopping node of Sandton City brands such as Rock Republic as well as the exclusive Evisu brand may be found here.

### Morningside Shopping Centre
Corner of Rivonia Road and Outspan Road, Morningside
Tel: 087 940 3833
www.morningsideshops.co.za
Open: daily, 9am–6pm (5pm Sat/Sun)

As one of Jo'burg's newest developments, Morningside Shopping Centre was developed on an owner-invested and operated model. The concept is based around the more bespoke boutiques where the buyers can personally interact with the boutique owners and, in some cases, the designers giving a highly personalised touch. Some 80 retailers are available inside, as well as a variety of restaurants to recharge your batteries at after a hard day pounding the pavement.

**Extreme Eyewear**  shades are obligatory in Jo'burg, Paul Smith, Marc Jacobs and Bottega Veneta all offer to preserve your eyesight and keep you looking super-cool in the African sun.

**Infinite 63**  opened by two edgy entrepreneurs with an eye for style, Infinite 63 sells luxury denim brands such as True Religion and G Star. Heavy antique doors lead into impressive interiors complete with exposed brickwork on the walls, wooden flooring underfoot and dangling lights overhead.

**Pana**  owned and operated by a Greek designer, European flair is evident throughout the fabulous range of shirts, dresses and trousers on offer at Pana. Blouses with bell sleeves, fringed dresses and satin waistcoats are Pana's signature pieces – so snap them up before somebody else does.

**Rene Mariane**  label-lovers flock to this store for designer Irena Staneva's sophisticated garments. Think beautiful silk blouses with pulled-in waists, daring bodices over shirts and high-waisted skirts. Posh clothes for posh people.

**Si Belle**  run by owners with a love of the tropics, Si Belle specialises in lightweight clothing made from cottons and linens. With everything imported from places such as Tahiti and Los Angeles, customers can expect intricate embroidery and bold prints on a range of summer garments. Accessorise accordingly with a white-sand beach.

**Smith & Olive** a range of beautifully handmade wooden toys for children (and their parents) to coo over. Wooden rocking horses and woollen animals will make childhood memories come flooding back.

**Nelson Mandela Square**
Nelson Mandela Square is appropriately named after the six-metre statue of the former president that stands tall in its centre.

**Penhaligon's** luxurious bottled fragrances and accessories are displayed on varnished wooden surfaces at Penhaligon's

**The Space** a sanctuary for South African designers, The Space celebrates individual style with rails upon rails of unusual one-off pieces.

**Original Penguin** a full lifestyle brand selling the very best in mens hats, polo shirts, classic cut shirts, shoes, knits and ties. Original Penguin describes its clientele as being a man with great style, intellect and humour. Sounds like us!

**La Bohem** a wide range of international clothing from stylish French vests to sophisticated Italian gowns

**Young Designers Emporium** renowned among consumers as one of Jo'burg (and indeed South Africa's) best shopping destinations to discover the latest (reasonably priced) fashion trends showcasing local talent

**Sandton City**
Sandton Drive and Rivonia Road, Sandton
Tel: 011 217 6000
www.sandton-city.co.za
Open: 9am-6pm Mon–Sat; 10am-4pm Sun

Located in Sandton – where else? - Sandton City is Jo'burg's largest shopping centre with over 300 stores for the browsing. Mixing high-end international brands with local boutiques, this mall will have even the most stubborn tightwad maxing out the credit card. Sandton City also has a tax-refund centre for visitors – meaning there'll be more money in your pocket to indulge with.

**Armani** classic Italian design a world away from the avenues of Milan, shoppers can't get enough of Giorgio – and quite rightly so

**Cartier** luxury jeweller and watch manufacturer was first introduced into the South African market at this very store, and it shows. Standards are maintained from the moment you enter, with strawberries and Champagne on offer and assistants with white gloves showing off the very latest bling. For your safety (and peace of mind), Sandton City also provides an escort when purchasing jewellery from any of its high-end stores.

**Castello** no outfit is ever truly complete without the perfect pair of designer heels, and nowhere knows this better than Castello. Known as the only place to shop for those serious about shoes, it's hardly surprising that this high-end store is brimming with

Sandton's poutiest fashionistas. Castello also carries a wide range of sizes, meaning women with both small and large tootsies can find the perfect fit.

**Guess** what's another store when you have more than 1,000 dotted across the globe? This Guess outlet is no less stylish than its siblings, offering fans of the brand a range of its handbags, shoes, belts and clothing.

**Louis Vuitton** needing little introduction, Louis Vuitton is conveniently situated across from Cartier and offers luscious leather accessories for designer-conscious ladies and gents. The interiors are pretty damn swish, too.

**Mango** aiming at young, urban women, this Spanish fashion house offers women everything they need for both work and play - from everyday essentials right through to eye-catching eveningwear.

**Mont Blanc** as the Rolls Royce of writing implements, wordsmiths can expect to find only the poshest pens alongside a range of watches, jewellery and eyewear at this beautiful branch

**Polo** – posh polo shirts are what Ralph Lauren does best, which is why the shelves at its dedicated shop in Sandton City positively strain under their multi-coloured weight. With every shade in the spectrum on offer, as well as caps, hats, shoes, belts and accessories, you'll be ready to hit the green looking pretty damn pristine in no time.

**The French Shop** – ooh, la, la! This saucy store boasts a range of eye-popping lingerie and sleepwear from France and beyond.

# Parkhurst & Saxonwold

One of Jo'burg's most stylish suburbs is Parkhurst, offering European-style shopping with rows of coffee shops, bars, restaurants and boutiques lining the paved street. Unique concept stores and designer shops jostle alongside one another for prime position, with well-heeled locals swanning in and out of stores takeaway coffee in-hand.

**Paul Smith** the one and only standalone Paul Smith shop in South Africa is well worth a visit, if not for its awe-inspiring aesthetics alone. Located inside a former house, the British designer's clothes and accessories are spread across two fabulous floors that cleverly incorporate Smith's signature stripes into the interior design.

**Willowbrook** undoubtedly one of Jo'burg's best children's shops, Willowbrook is a haven of beautiful children's clothes, toys and accessories. It also prides itself on being sellers of Phoebe & Floyd, an internationally renowned children's label.

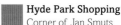 **Hyde Park Shopping**
Corner of Jan Smuts and 6th Avenue
Tel: 011 325 4340

www.hydeparkshopping.co.za
Open: 9am–6pm Mon–Sat
'Life's a gift. Label it', so says the tagline at Hyde Park Shopping centre, a fully-enclosed mall that offers countless brands to spend your hard-earned cash on inside. As Jo'burg's landmark retail complex, it has everything any one shopaholic could ever need.

**11 Elves** much sought-after European brands such as Petit Bateau find their home in this beautiful children's clothing boutique. Snap up some bits and bobs for the little ones back home.

**2A** Bottega Veneta, Christian Dior, Louis Vuitton and Alberta Ferretti are just some of the designer names folded neatly on the shelves of 2A. So whether you'd addicted to bags, hooked on shoes or obsessed with clothes, be sure to bring your credit card.

**Cottage Flowers** candy-striped boxes and polka-dot ribbons add a little something to the floral displays at Cottage Flowers, offering beautiful bouquets for your home and loved ones

**Hoy P'loy –** a florist that treats its florals more like precious artworks than anything else.

**Hyde Park Personal Shopping** personal shopping adds a touch of panache to any retail outing, and the superstar service at Hyde Park Shopping centre is no exception. Tailored to fit in with all tastes and any budget, the service can be enjoyed over the phone or in person and can help with a range of dilemmas – from finding a present to finding a whole new look.

**Jo Malone** flagship store in South Africa, customers here can expect the brand's signature black and cream interiors and all its usual high-end products

**Max Mara** spacious shop makes the tailored clothes look as if they are displayed on a stage rather than shelves

**Orpheo Brothers** the Orpheo twins are renowned in Jo'burg for one-off pieces that truly dazzle. Their edgy jewellery incorporates semi-precious stones and unusual elements such as leather.

**Ruby & The Dust** eye-catching white surfaces entice shoppers through the doors at Ruby & The Dust, while the store's magnificent costume jewellery practically sells itself.

**X-Section** all manner of designer duds to deck yourself out in, from True Religion to Rock & Republic

 **The Mall of Rosebank**
Between Bath Avenue and Cradock Avenue, Rosebank
Tel: 011 788 5530
www.themallofrosebank.co.za

The Mall of Rosebank has become synonymous with eclectic, somewhat artistic tenants. South African brands such as Stoned Cherie can be found here, together with a host of other shops, a number of restaurants, a weekly rooftop flea market and an art house cinema showcasing mainly independent movies.

shop…

**Attitude** designer costume jewellery and accessories from around the world – a great range of all hats, belts, bags and scarves

**Banana Moon** one of Johannesburg's leading suppliers of designer swimming costumes including beachwear and accessories

**Café Cotton** fine men's shirts, cufflinks and ties crafted since the 19th century. The extensive selection of shirts is available in both the French cuff or the barrel shirt cuff

**Ed Hardy** biker chic is brought to Jo'burg at Ed Hardy, offering tattoo-inspired t-shirts, hoodies and hats for the daring dresser.

**Gucci** – legendary Italian fashion brand with a show-stopping window display, gilded gold doors and rails of the finest designer duds

**Palazzo Pitti** designer Italian and Spanish shoes as well as sought after Dissona bags and accessories

**Paloma** high end womenswear, eveningwear, business suits and little dancing dresses as well as hats and accessories. In store alterations and a made to measure service to ensure that all clientele are perfectly fitted.

**The Space** unusual dresses, skirts, pants and shirts for the more eclectic and stylish shopper

**Sun Goddess** high end African fashion. Rich, bold African prints and details are incorporated into bodices, skirts and shirts.

# Illovo

Bordering Hyde Park, Sandhurst and Craighall Park, the suburb of Illovo shouldn't be overlooked as a shopping destination with a number of stores surrounding its main square.

**Chocolate de Belgique** a boutique chocolaterie based, where fine Belgian chocolates are hand made on the premises by chocolatiers. There are opportunities to indulge in a chocolate tasting and making evening and a great selection of chocolates with fillings including chilli, crème caramel, coffee to take away.

**La Perla** internationally recognised as the leaders in luxurious lingerie, La Perla doesn't need to do much to flog its risqué wares. But a store discretely located in Illovo Square certainly doesn't hurt, especially if gentlemen shoppers have anything to do with it.

**Thrupps** often compared to the likes of Harrods Food Emporium Thrupps sells the very best in food. Imported chocolates, French pates, Italian meats and Greek olives are among the foods on display. The famous Thrupps hampers provide a perfect and unique gift and they provide a reliable delivery service

 **Birdhaven**

**Eclectic Gifts** a new addition to Birdhaven, Eclectic Gifts sells magnificent tablewear including oversized paper napkins, embroidered table cloths and stylish place mats as well as beautiful glass and silverware.

### Blubird Shopping Centre

A good addition to the Jo'burg shopping centre scene Bluebird Shopping Centre makes interesting use of space placing fabulous little shops in corners and nooks creating interesting and welcoming spaces

**Le Bijou** stocking beautiful gifts including finery and glassware as well as an extensive selection of richly coloured jewellery and accessories

**Helon Melon** proudly South African Helon Melon sells 100% cotton linen and bedding in a variety of prints, colours and styles

**Claudia His and Hers** iconic fashion including the likes of the William Rust and Rich & Skinny denim collections by fashion icons Joie Rucker and Michael Glasser as well as Emperor's New Clothes.

**Tam Tam** Collection rich furnishings, crystal chandeliers and soft hangings create a display space for only the finest in French lingerie and swimwear, the Tam Tam Collection epitomises style and femininity

### Melrose Arch
The High Street, Melrose North
Tel: 011 684 0002
www.melrosearch.co.za
Open: daily, 9am-6pm (4pm Sun)

A fusion of office, retail, leisure and residential space, Melrose Arch is a hub of social activity. Shopping here is in the form of a carefully crafted European-style high street, complete with a piazza bursting with restaurants and a hotel to check into should you want to rest your weary head after a hard day's spending.

**L'Occitane** – offering an extensive range of fragrances and skincare products, made from natural ingredients and inspired by the 'art de vivre'

**Tiger of Sweden** – ranging from sharp suits to chic casual wear, this outlet has every occasion sorted. Fashion-forward and trendy, it's no wonder its clothes are worn by the likes of The Hives and Kaiser Chiefs. Imitation, as they say, is the sincerest form of flattery.

# play...

Hedonists love to play – more so, say, than work. Which is why we've compiled the best places to play in Jo'burg, from heartstopping adventures for adrenaline junkies to relaxing activities for pleasure seekers. Whatever your favourite form of fun, you're sure to find it in this city of cool.

Blessed with one of the best climates in Africa, it's hardly surprising that many of Jo'burg's pleasurable pursuits are based around othe great outdoors, with sport often top of the agenda. Rugby, cricket, golf and polo are national treasures, and visitors should definitely try and get in on the action – if not playing, than watching from the sidelines with a glass of suitably chilled Champers in-hand. As a chance to mingle with the city's upper classes watch polo at the Inanda Club ,you're sure to be kept in the company to which you've undoubtedly become accustomed; locals love it, and so will you.

Golf, in particular, is hot property here; those who can afford the green fees wile away the hours on sun-soaked fairways, but be warned – some courses are so exclusive they can seem impenetrable. Which is why we've found services that admit you with ease without you having to battle your way past surly-faced gate-keepers. Organising everything from tee-off times to caddies, these companies

leave you stress-free to enjoy a round at places such as the Glendower Golf Club and the Royal Johannesburg & Kensington Golf Club, among others. Indeed, there are more than enough courses to keep you and your nine iron entertained; dump your other half off at the clubhouse and enjoy. You deserve it.

Those who prefer their pursuits a little more fast-paced might like to book a trip high above Jo'burg in a helicopter or hot air balloon, or perhaps take a leap of faith from the Orlando Towers in Soweto with just a rubber cord stopping you from plummeting to your death. Abseiling and skydiving can also be arranged in Jo'burg, so those who like to live life in the fast lane can teeter on the edge to their heart's content.

Sport isn't the only way to play in Jo'burg, either. Relaxing is big business in the city that sleeps a little too much, with stylish spas to stop stressed-out city workers from snapping. We all like to be treated like royalty now and again, and the resorts in Jo'burg do just that with a range of world-class treatments to rest, relax and rejuvenate even the most wound-up visitors. Highly recommended are Mangwanani and Life Day Spa, two of our own personal favourites.

However you choose to get your kicks, rest assured that you'll be able to do it in Jo'burg. And do it in true superstar style, no less.

*play...*

# Ballooning

### Bill Harrop's "Original" Balloon Safaris

Tel: 011 705 3201
www.balloon.co.za

If you dream of hot air ballooning high above the South African plains, then Bill Harrop is your man – so to speak – and looks like the kind of colonial character you'd imagine to live here (white beard and all). Offering flights across the Magalies River Valley, the Cradle of Humankind, Bela-Bela and Waterberg, guests can hop in a basket and explore Jo'burg and all its surrounds via spectacular bird's eye view. For a truly magical experience, book a sunrise or sunset flight, quaff Champers and drift lazily over the majestic Magliesberg Mountain Range. Up, up and away!

**Flight Areas:** Magalies River Valley, Cradle of Humankind, Bela-Bela, Waterberg

# Bungee jumping

### Orlando Towers

Dynamo Street, Corner of
Old Potch Road, Orlando, Soweto
Tel: 012 345 5114 / 071 674 4343
www.orlandotowers.co.za
Open: 10am 'til sunset Fri–Sun

The two colourful cooling towers that rise out of the ground in Soweto are the largest landmarks in the area, and Orlando Towers uses them to its advantage by throwing people off the top of them – attached to rubber cords, of course. The company offers a range of terror-inducing activities, including traditional bungee jumping, power swinging, internal swinging and abseiling – anything, in fact, that will turn your skin from boring beige to gross green. The less adventurous can, however, take the lift to the top for stunning 360-degree views of Soweto. Sometimes it's better to watch.

# Canopy tours

### Magaliesberg Canopy Tours

Magaliesberg
Tel: 014 535 0150
www.magaliescanopytour.co.za

If you like to be in the very thick of things than Magaliesberg Canopy Tours can help you get up close and personal with one of the oldest mountain ranges in the world – 2,500 million years old, to be precise. With eleven platforms built against the rock face of Ysterhout Kloof, you'll slide from one platform to another via steel cables while taking in jaw-dropping views of the gorge. Just don't look down.

# Fly fishing

### Intrepid Fly

Sandton
Tel: 083 657 2255
www.intrepidfly.com

There's nothing more satisfying than catching your own dinner – or at least trying to – which is why a fly fishing trip with is an ego-boosting way to spend an afternoon. Offering you the chance to catch a local species called yellow fish, Intrepid Fly will take you into the teeming waters of the Vaal River to see if you've got what it takes to hook a winner.

# Golf

### Glendower Golf Club
20 Marais Road
Tel: 011 453 1013/4
www.glendower.co.za

One of Jo'burg's most picturesque courses with 18 holes spread across kikuyu grass-covered fairways, Glendower Golf Club would impress even the most die-hard golf enthusiast. Lush vegetation and wildlife abounds here, which is why the club was proclaimed a conservation area in the 70s and has been voted one of the ten best courses in South Africa.

### Royal Johannesburg & Kensington Golf Club
1 Fairway Avenue, Linksfield North, Gauteng
Tel: 011 640 3021
www.royaljk.za.rom

The name says it all; regal in every sense of the word, Royal Johannesburg & Kensington Golf Club is prestige personified – having hosted seven South African Opens and a roster of other major tournaments. Comprising two world-class 18-hole courses – the East Course and the West Course – as well as a chic clubhouse and restaurant for relaxing in afterwards, this is golf at its most gorgeous and green.

### SAGolfing.com
Randburg
Tel: 011 706 6869 / 082 770 1733
www.sagolfing.com

With so many courses to choose from it can be hard to know where to tee-off in Jo'burg. But fear not, for SAGolfing. com is at-hand to help you with all your golfing concerns; offering services such as confirming tee-off times at courses, golf club hire and transportation, the website draws on its vast database of contacts in the city to make sure your time on Jo'burg's most gorgeous greens is as good as it should be. And if you can take constructive criticism, then the company can arrange for a professional to follow you around the course and offer advice on sharpening up your game. Just put down the golf club if they get too personal.

# Helicopter flight

### Bassair Aviation
No. 8 Bellevue
129 Nicola Street, Wonderboom
Tel: 082 892 9444 / 082 928 8090
www.bassair-aviation.co.za

If you've got your head in the clouds most of the time then let Bassair Aviation sweep you off your feet; the company offers practical helicopter charters to help you get from A to B without fear of being stuck in traffic-choked streets. After all, why be crammed into a sweaty four-by-four with no air-conditioning when you could be slicing through the sky in half the time? Operating throughout South Africa, those visiting Jo'burg will be pleased to hear

*play…*

that Bassair Aviation has a base at nearby Wonderboom Airport – with a fabulous fleet that's yours for the taking. Nice choppers indeed.

**Sunwa River Lodge**
Parys
Tel: 082 651 1960
www.sunwa.co.za

Seen all the Vietnam movies? Never forgotten the opening scene of A-Team? If you've always dreamed of flying in an American war machine then Sunwa River Lodge can make your dreams come true with Huey helicopter flights. Perfect for boys who love their toys, the lodge will strap you into one of its cool choppers and have you soaring the sky in no time. The pilot will even demonstrate simulated combat flights over the Vaal River for those feeling particularly childish. The less adventurous, however, can opt for more serene scenic flights and soak up the sweeping views below.

# Horse racing

**Turffontein Racecourse**
Turf Club Street, Turffontein
Tel: 011 681 150

Those into horseplay will fall head over hooves for Turffontein Racecourse, built in 1887 and now one of South Africa's oldest racecourses. Filled with fine fillies, the course boasts two turf tracks and hosts the Group One South African Derby and the Summer Cup. Hedge your bets and see how they run!

# Luxury car hire

**Status Luxury Vehicles**
Jo'burg
Tel: 011 468 3910
www.slv.co.za

There's nothing quite like being behind the wheel of a sexy supercar to make you feel like a superstar, and nobody knows this better than Status Luxury Vehicles. Offering flashy wheels from Ferraris to Bentleys, the high-end rental service enables you to tear down Jo'burg's roads with the best of 'em. And if you don't want to drive yourself, then you can opt for a chauffeur driven limousine to get you from hotel to hotspot in style.

# Microbrewery

**Gilroy's Brewery**
Ngwenya Glass Village,
Muldersdrift
Tel: 011 796 3020 / 076 040 7530
www.gilroybeers.co.za

For the microbrewer, creating a beer is pure passion; Gilroy's Brewery epitomises this, with beer-making something of an age-old art form here. Using only the finest natural ingredients – including the best hops, malt and yeast – this small operation offers visitors a glimpse into the beer-making process, and the chance to taste golden goodness unfiltered and free from preservatives. Taste the difference.

# Mountaineering

### GoVertical
Magaliesberg
Tel: 082 731 4696
www.govertical.co.za

Adrenaline junkies will find thrills aplenty at GoVertical, a South African adventure company specialising in Jo'burg's natural peaks and troughs. Whether climbing up mountains or abseiling down gorges, GoVertical offers excursions to the likes of Mount Kilimanjaro and the Cradle of Humankind to those looking to, er, get their rocks off. Highly recommending is 'kloofing' – an activity that involves making your way down a water system (complete with rapids and waterfalls) without a boat. If that doesn't get your blood pumping, we don't know what will!

# Plane charter

### Naturelink Aviation
Wonderboom Airport
Tel: 012 543 3448
www.naturelink.co.za

Private jets aren't just for the privileged few, as Naturelink Aviation demonstrates. Visitors can use the company to charter an impressive roster of jets and navigate the skies in true superstar style, direct form Wonderboom Airport. Whether cruising for pleasure, business or simple for safari, then sky really is the limit.

# Polo

### Inanda Club
1 Forrest Road, Inanda,
Sandton
Tel: 011 884 1414
www.inandaclub.co.za

Polo is much-loved in South Africa, with posh supporters of the sport flocking in their well-heeled droves to the Inanda Club to watch the action unfold in the heart of Sandton. Exciting equestrian displays and the chance to mingle with the upper echelons of society (and climb a rung of two of the social ladder while you're at it), make a sun-drenched afternoon at the Inanda Club an extremely good idea indeed.

# Skydiving

### Adventure Skydives
Carletonville Airport
Tel: 083 949 7894
www.adventureskydives.com

While hurtling towards the ground may not be everyone's cup of tea, those who do get a kick out of vertical velocity should head to Adventure Skydives. While it has outposts dotted throughout Jo'burg, we recommend Carletonville Airport for the best jumps in town. Stepping out of a plane solo may be a little intimidating for some, which is where Adventure Skydive's trained instructors come in handy for assisted tandem jumps. Strapped to someone that knows what they're doing, all you have to do is enjoy the ride and not worry about pulling any pesky cords. The drop-zone facilities aren't bad,

play...

either, with a snack bar and picnic tables to enjoy lunch on – just make sure you eat after your jump.

# Spas

### Life Day Spa
Design Quarter District,
Fourways
Tel: 011 465 7777
www.lifedayspa.co.za

Spread across 1,500-square-metres, Life Day Spa proves that size does, in fact, matter. As well as housing Terenzo, one of Jo'burg's best hair salons for ladies who love their locks, the spa also comprises a number of different treatment rooms, a heated pool, steam rooms, saunas and Swiss showers – and that's just for starters. Treatments on offer here include massages, facials and manicures, using only high-end product ranges such as La Prairie, Guinot and Dermalogica. Come and be pampered within an inch of your life.

### Mangwanani
Indaba, William Nicol Drive, Fourways
Tel: 011 840 6600
www.mangwanani.co.za

Found at the Indaba Hotel, this outlet of the prestigious Mangwanani spa chain is just as chic as its other branches. With its décor unmistakably African, the spa combines Western facilities with traditional techniques – a formula that has helped it win 'Spa of the Year' for the last four years running. Guests here are greeted with drums and Champagne before changing into robes and

slippers and indulging in a variety of rejuvenating treatments. With a range of treatments on offer, including facials and massages, Mangwanani is sure to make even the most discerning spa-goers feel like African aristocracy. Highly recommended is the Moonlight Night Spa package, which enables guests to enjoy treatments under the cover of darkness.

### The Saxon Spa and Studio
36 Saxon Road, Sandhurst
Tel: 011 292 6000
www.thesaxon.com

Located within the gated confines of a gorgeous boutique hotel (see Sleep) in Sandhurst, the Saxon Spa and Studio is the perfect place to come for a little rest and relaxation. The interiors are decked out in contemporary African décor, while the spa itself comprises a number of treatment gazebos and water facilities, amongst others. The spa's signature, however, is the sound therapy room; using gongs, cymbals, singing bowls and bells, the room offers a complete holistic experience to stressed-out clients. Treatments on offer include all the usual facials and massages.

### Skin Sense Day Spa
Rivonia, Sandton
Tel: 011 807 6281
www.skinsensedayspa.com

Focusing on touch, taste, smell, sound and sight, the Skin Sense Day Spa in Rivonia tailors its treatments towards re-awakening your senses – and boy does it work! Using a strictly holistic approach to its range of therapies, the spa caters to customers who don't have the time to head to a spa for a week at a time with scaled-down therapies that unwind even the most highly-strung of customers in just a few hours. Body wraps, facials and manicures make up more than 100 different treatments.

## Tours

### The Soweto Rhubuluza
Soweto
Tel: 011 463 8895
www.simkile.co.za

Bar crawls can be disastrous or damn good fun, and thankfully for this crawl the Soweto Rhubuluza falls into the latter category. Taking those who sign-up on a booze-fuelled tour of Soweto's taverns, the Soweto Rhubuluza is described as an 'edutainment experience of a lifetime' and allows tourists to soak up the local vibe without looking through the steamed-up windows of a tour bus. Historical sights are also included for culture vultures.

play...

notes...

# info...

**Dangers**

Jo'burg has long been regarded as one of the most dangerous cities in the world with crime statistics and stories you can t make up! I don't want to discourage your visit to South Africa, but be careful. That said, like any city, there are places to go to and there are places you avoid. When travelling at night, plan your route so as to avoid getting lost especially when visiting places in Braamfontein and Newtown. The township of Alexandra is also a bit loopy. Try not to take the London Road off the N3 from the airport through Alexandra.

One of the places in Jo'burg you are advised to avoid is the CBD, specifically Hillbrow. Home to illegal immigrants, drug lords, pimps and generally dubious characters, it is dangerous and vitually ungovernable sector in the city … "What?" you may be saying … drugs & women … you make that sound like a bad thing. Yes, here it is …get your kicks in Sandton!

South Africa doesn't have the plague of pick pockets as seen in Europe. What we do have that is a major problem is car-jacking. This is a serious crime issue for all to be aware of. Assailants will literally hold you up at a busy intersection in the middle of the day in from of hundreds of onlookers. This is usually dome with guns and can often result in a shooting. Keep your wits about you, remain alert to your surroundings, especially in unlit areas and keep your windows rolled up. Watch out for street vendors and beggars as they can be assailants in disguise.

Smash and grabs are another brazen crime that occurs at the busy intersections in broad daylight. Avoid leaving bags, cameras, lap tops or any items of perceived value on the seats of your car. The assailants will walk past the car, smash your window with a brick and remove its contents including jewellery off your body in the commotion.

**Internet**

South Africa has a good internet infrastructure, however the speeds are poor. All the hotels mentioned provide broadband and most on a wireless network.

## Money

The currency in South Africa is Rands (ZAR). A taxi trip into Sandton will cost around R400. At the time of going to print the Rand was worth $1 = R8, €1=R11 and £1=12. Credit cards and debit cards can be pretty much used anywhere, but it is still useful to carry cash for some of the smaller places.

## Public transport

You can't complain about the public transport because there isn't any! This has long been the joke. There is no underground / metro, there are no trams that wander through the city. A first class train service runs from the airport to Sandton. The bus system is a joke, while the informal taxi serviced runs well but is considered dangerous for travellers who are not familiar with it, unless of course you share with a registered guide. Rent a car, employ a chauffeur or call a cab!

## Rental Cars

There are several international agencies in South Africa. Arrange you rental car before arriving in South Africa. This is cheapest online. Please travel with your drivers licence as you will have to produce it before taking the car. You must also travel with it at all time as random roadblocks will demand to see a valid drivers licence.

## Taxis

Get used to them as they will be your primary mode of transport if you don't have a rental car. A suggestion is to get the name and number of the guy you first travel with. Try negotiating a deal where by he is your only driver and you call him when you need him. Set a rate and you will save a heap of cash. Taxis are expensive in Jo'burg. For example a trip from the airport to Sandton can cost from R350 – R600 depending who you get … Negotiate with these guys.

## Telephone

The international country code is +27; in the listings you will find the telephone numbers given are those to be dialled locally, if you are dialling from abroad you will need to remove the first 0 and add on the +27 to the front. Make sure you have your international roaming activated before you arrive or carry an old mobile phone with you and simply purchase a sim card on arrival (you will find a kiosk or two through arrivals).

## Tipping
The rules are pretty much the same as anywhere else on the planet, have a good meal, drink or coffee and leave the waiter a 10% tip. Some places have a service charge included so make sure to check or ask the wait staff. If you feel the service was particularly good a tip of 15–20% will always be well received. Porters expect a tip, depending on the size and number of bags, a tip of around R20 should suffice. Want a few special in-room requests then grease the hands of the concierge on arrival. For taxi drivers round off the bill to leave them something, whereas chauffeurs will want a tip for each journey, so bank on about 10% of the net rate.

## Weather
Jo'burg has one of the best climates in the world, with 4 seasons. Summer months are from November till March with average temperatures from 15–30°C. The rainy season in Johannesburg is during the summer months (opposite in Cape Town). Generally this involves hot days, with afternoon showers. These showers can be large electric thunderstorms. The winter months are dry, and temperatures can drop to 0 degrees, but generally average at 8–16°C. It doesn't snow in Johannesburg, but the snow on the Drakensberg will contribute to colder days in Jo'burg.

# index...

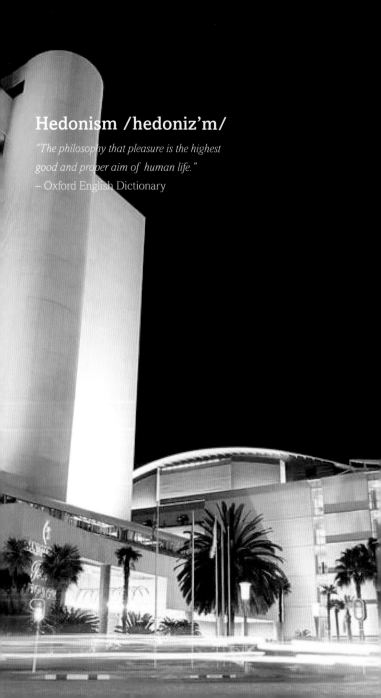

# Hedonism /hedoniz'm/

*"The philosophy that pleasure is the highest good and proper aim of human life."*
– Oxford English Dictionary

## Hg2 Corporate

### Branded Gifts....

Looking for a corporate gift with real value? Want to reinforce your company's presence at a conference or event? We can provide you with branded guides so recipients will explore their chosen city with your company's logo right under their nose.

Branding can go from a small logo discreetly embossed on to our standard cover, to a fully custom jacket in your company's colours and in a material of your choice. We can also include a letter from your CEO/Chairman/President and add or remove as much or as little other content as you require. We can create a smaller, 'best of' guide, branded with your company's livery in a format of your choice. Custom guides can also be researched and created from scratch to any destination not yet on our list.

For more information, please contact Ben at ben@hg2.com

### Content licensing....

We can also populate your own website or other materials with our in-depth content, superb imagery and insider knowledge.

For more information, please contact Tremayne at tremayne@hg2.com

## Hg-Who?

Welcome to the world of Hg2 – the UK's leading luxury city guide series. Launched in 2004 as the *A Hedonist's guide to…* series, we are pleased to announce a new look to our guides, now called simply Hg2. In response to customer feedback, the new Hg2 is 25% lighter, even more luxurious to look at or touch, and flexible, for greater portability. However, fear not, our content is still as meticulously researched and well-illustrated as ever and the spirit of hedonism still infuses our work. Our brand of hedonism taps into the spirit of 'Whatever Works for You' – from chic boutique hotels to well-kept-secret restaurants, to the very best cup of coffee in town. We do not mindlessly seek out the most expensive; instead, we search high and low for the very best each city has to offer.

So take Hg2 as your companion to a city. Written by well-regarded journalists and constantly updated online at www.Hg2.com (register this guide to get one year of free access), it will help you Sleep, Eat, Drink, Shop, Party and Play like a sophisticated local.

*"Hg2 is about foreign life as art"* **Vanity Fair**
*"The new travel must-haves"* **Daily Telegraph**
*"Insight into what's really going on"* **Tatler**
*"A minor bible"* **New York Times**
*"Excellent guides for stylish travellers"* **Harper's Bazaar**
*"Discerning travellers, rejoice!"* **Condé Nast Traveller**